"Those in spiritual warfare circles often hear about the spirits of Jezebel, religion and witchcraft. But few people connect the dots between these three with the insight Jennifer LeClaire offers in this book. By exposing these demonic forces one by one with the light of biblical truth, she unveils how they operate both individually and collectively. More importantly, she equips mature believers to combat and overcome darkness through the power of God."

Marcus Yoars, former editor, Charisma magazine

"In her powerful new book, *Satan's Deadly Trio*, Jennifer LeClaire gives depth and clarity for the believer's most powerful teaching. I could hear the bells of freedom ringing as I read every page. The spirits of Jezebel, witchcraft and religion choke the life out of believers and power out of the Church. Her chapters on the spirit of Ahab and the spirit of Jehu are new and fresh. This book gives clear direction on how to fight and war against these demonic strongholds. This book will assist pastors, teachers and the laity in teaching and living at a higher level of freedom."

Ron Phillips, senior pastor, Abba's House; author;
television and radio host

"In unique description and presentation, Jennifer clearly exposes the root of pride, self-righteousness and legalism that desires to manipulate and control rather than liberate and empower. She also guides us into the path of freedom through the weapon of forgiveness and release. The candor and directness by which Jennifer unpacks the message in this book is commendable. She encourages us to expose the façades and gloss, and to take honest review. May we recognize the deadly trio and unholy trinity that would keep us constrained from the glorious plans of God for us. May we keep our eyes fixed on Jesus."

Doug Stringer, Turning Point Ministries International;
Somebody Cares International

T0311014

Books by Jennifer LeClaire

Satan's DEADLY TRIO

DEFEATING THE DECEPTIONS OF
JEZEBEL, RELIGION AND WITCHCRAFT

JENNIFER LeCLAIRE

Chosen
a division of Baker Publishing Group
Minneapolis, Minnesota

Published by Chosen Books
11400 Hampshire Avenue South
Bloomington, Minnesota 55438
www.chosenbooks.com

Chosen Books is a division of
Baker Publishing Group, Grand Rapids, Michigan

Printed in the United States of America

Library of Congress Cataloging-in-Publication Data
LeClaire, Jennifer (Jennifer L.)
    Satan's deadly trio : defeating the deceptions of Jezebel, religion, and witchcraft / Jennifer LeClaire.
        pages cm
    Includes index.
    Summary: "Discover how the sinister spirits of Jezebel, Religion, and Witchcraft work together to derail your Kingdom purpose. Incisive insight and strategic battle tactics will overcome them"—Provided by publisher.
    ISBN 978-0-8007-9589-4 (pbk. : alk. paper) 1. Spiritual warfare. 2. Jezebel, Queen, consort of Ahab, King of Israel. 3. Religion—Controversial literature. 4. Witchcraft. I. Title.
BV4509.5.L443 2014
235'.4—dc23   2014018270

Cover design by LOOK Design Studio

This book is dedicated to the real Trinity

—Father, Son and Holy Spirit—

who helped me expose the wiles
of the enemy for His glory.
His Word equips us with the weapons
of warfare that allow us to enforce
Christ's victory here on earth.

Thank You, Father, for sending Jesus
to disarm principalities and powers.

Thank You, Jesus, for conquering death,
hell and the grave.

Thank You, Holy Spirit, for leading and guiding me
into all truth about who I am in Christ
and my authority in Him.

Contents

Foreword

There are few people mentioned in Scripture as wicked as Jezebel. Her name has become synonymous with *rebellion*, *witchcraft* and *seduction*. She hated the God of Israel, promoted idolatry throughout the covenant nation and seduced the people of God into apostasy.

Jezebel was very religious. She was devoted to Baal, and was used by demons to recruit and force others to worship idols. Religion and witchcraft operate together, and these spirits are being exposed through this book. Every believer needs to be educated in this area. We cannot be ignorant of how Jezebel, witchcraft and religion work together to enslave and destroy the lives of many.

Jezebel was controlled by demons, and she released a horde of evil spirits throughout the land. The nation of Israel became demonized as a result of her rebellion and was judged for her witchcraft and whoredom.

God used the prophet Elijah to contend with Jezebel. It is not surprising that one of the strongest prophets in Israel's history came at a time of the greatest danger. We need prophetic insight and revelation in contending with these dark spirits, and Jennifer LeClaire has answered this call to be a prophetic voice to this generation. Her insight into how Jezebel works is as much needed today as it was in the days of Elijah. I have seen families and ministries devastated by the influence of Jezebel and related spirits. It is heartbreaking to see immorality, control, division and witchcraft destroy the lives of people who seem to be defenseless in stopping the destruction caused by Satan's minions. Thank God for today's prophetic voices who will raise up a standard against the works of darkness.

Jennifer LeClaire has been given an assignment to expose the works of Jezebel and other spirits that work together to destroy the lives of people. Her experience in contending with these unholy spirits will help those in similar situations overcome and receive victory.

A lack of discernment in dealing with problems can be very frustrating. Insight and understanding will help believers overcome the strategies of hell and achieve victories and breakthroughs. God does not want us ignorant of Satan's devices and wiles. The church needs the information in this book. Pastors and leaders need this information. Prophets and intercessors need this information. I highly recommend this book and welcome it as an additional resource to believers everywhere.

This book is a revelation of how Jezebel works with religion and witchcraft to hinder the Church from moving forward and advancing the Kingdom. Satan hates light and truth. Light and truth will disarm and defeat the agenda of hell. We are living in a day of increased understanding and revelation. The saints are arising with a new understanding of the spirit realm. We will see more breakthroughs today and in the years to come as a result of this increased knowledge. We are now disarming and stopping the works of darkness through prayer and deliverance. I believe that multitudes of people will be released from captivity as a result of books like this that expose the works of darkness.

As you read this book, do it prayerfully with humility. Let your faith be stirred to do exploits, and let your wisdom in spiritual warfare increase. Let the insights from this book open a new chapter in your life, and let your future be filled with victory after victory and breakthrough after breakthrough in the name of the Lord Jesus Christ.

John Eckhardt, apostle and overseer,
Crusaders Church, Chicago; founder,
IMPACT Network and Apostolic
Institute of Ministry (AIM)

Acknowledgments

I am grateful to Chosen Books for allowing me this platform to expose *Satan's Deadly Trio* with scriptural reference and practical experience. Thanks to Jane Campbell, editorial director of Chosen Books, and my book editor, Ann Weinheimer, for laboring with me to present this revelation and information with clarity.

I am grateful to those who have walked with me through the spiritual warfare that came against me while writing this book, like Robin, Esther, Mary-Alice, Ruth and Jim. And I appreciate all those who first taught me about these spirits and gave me the inspiration to dig below the surface to see the deeper evils—then expose them.

1

The Unholy Trinity

I had been on the mission field in one-hundred-degree weather in a nation known for its false gospel for more than a week— and battling principalities and powers every step of the way. Laboring to take the Good News to a nation where the spirit of Jezebel wields an especially wicked influence brings an onslaught against your mind and sometimes even unpleasant manifestations in your body. I was not wrestling against flesh and blood, but it sure felt as though I had been in a heavyweight boxing match at the end of some days.

Granted, I was unprepared for the level of spiritual warfare I would encounter in a nation where the effects of witchcraft regularly make headlines. And I was not yet acquainted with the way the religious spirit impels us into morphing the image of Jesus from One who delivers to One who demands superhuman performance to find His favor.

Indeed, I had no idea how Jezebel, the spirit of religion and witchcraft work together to put us in bondage, strip us of our God-given identity and derail our Kingdom purpose. But I would soon get a firsthand lesson from what I call a deadly trio—the spirits of Jezebel, religion and witchcraft—that I will never forget.

When immature or inexperienced believers enter harvest fields that strongly oppose the Gospel, the dynamics are ripe for this unholy trinity to wreak havoc on the whole evangelistic endeavor. This is because these participants, though willing to minister, are not usually trained to guard their hearts and minds against high-level spiritual attacks.

Indeed, even experienced warriors can fall prey to the workings of Jezebel, religion and witchcraft in Gospel-hostile nations. I have seen missionaries in heated arguments over who will maintain possession of the room key during day-trips. I have watched full-blown strife in the midst of a vote to decide whether the team's bus will stop at a restaurant so famished people can eat or go back to the mission base so exhausted people can rest. And I have witnessed plenty of unhealthy competition over who gets to use the microphone at outreaches. Of course, I have also seen God move for His glory despite the fleshly or childish mindsets, because it is not His will that any should perish (see 2 Peter 3:9).

The point is, however, that the potential demonic inroads to our souls are real—and alarming. No one can submit to the flesh and submit to the Holy Spirit at the same time. The works of the flesh are especially wicked—and when we sow to the flesh we reap corruption (see Galatians 6:8). *The Amplified Bible* says we will "reap decay and ruin and destruction."

This deadly trio of Jezebel, religion and witchcraft stirs up the flesh, tapping in to tired bodies, hungry stomachs, prideful tendencies in our souls, as well as traditional mindsets that have not been renewed. As a young believer on my first mission trip, I was not prepared for these dark attacks.

If you run in spiritual warfare circles, you have no doubt battled the spirits of Jezebel, religion and witchcraft. But until you receive the discernment to distinguish the subtle working of each individual enemy—and until you get a revelation of how these three spirits work together to hold people in bondage—you are not fully equipped for war.

In this chapter, I will expose the prophetic partnership of this deadly trio: Jezebel, religion and witchcraft. In brief, the Bible speaks of Israel's Queen Jezebel and "her witchcrafts" (2 Kings 9:22 NASB). We know from the account of her life in Scripture that she was religious—even if her religion was false. By the end of this chapter, you will have a solid foundation on how this unholy alliance works to steal, kill and destroy God's plan for your life, so that you can prepare for victory in your next battle against these spirits.

The Subtlety of Witchcraft

The danger in any spiritual warfare teaching is sending students running off with new revelation based on partial understanding. When that happens, you are in danger of buffeting the air—or provoking another enemy to attack without ever dealing with the first enemy. In other words, while you are busy dealing with the wrong spirit, the spirit you need to battle continues its assault against your mind. With that understanding, let's get more clarity on how these spirits work together.

During my first experience on the mission field, I managed to avoid strife over room keys, pit stops and other potential conflicts inherent in large missions trips in a country where Jezebel rules. I failed, however, to realize the impact that this trio was having on my mind.

17

Despite being trained and equipped to combat forces of darkness, I was actually fighting only half the battle. I focused on binding evil in the atmosphere, but failed to guard my own heart in the inner battle against my mind.

The subtle attack started with "religious" thoughts about how I was doing more work than everyone else and no one appreciated it—or even noticed. In one sense, this was true, and that fact gave me plenty of grist for this demon-inspired mill. I was up two hours before the rest of the team on some days. I did not stop for lunch with the rest of the team on many days. And I ran around the city or stood on my feet during team rest periods on most days.

A humble heart, one that was ministering these things out of generous service, would reject such a "religious" thought at its inception. Instead, my soul meditated on this "injustice" every day for more than a week, as I wore myself out performing the work of the ministry.

This is a good example of how subtle the enemy can be. He does not need to tell you a full-blown lie to bind you. The devil can bind you with partial truth by twisting your perspective. He does this by shining the light on your wants and your needs, effectively distracting you from God's will and provision of grace for the work He has called you to do.

This shows the partnership the spirit of religion has with another member of the trio, witchcraft. Religion plants thoughts in your mind, and then witchcraft magnifies them, blowing them out of proportion.

Religious witchcraft can also cause physical manifestations of sickness—fatigue, weariness and slumber are key manifestations. I went through a season earlier in my walk with God when I was learning about this spirit in which I literally slept my way to this revelation. Every day, I would battle witchcraft with a rote prayer. Every day, witchcraft hit me back. And every day I ended up sleeping halfway through the morning.

When I finally made the connection, I stopped praying those rote prayers and asked the Lord for discernment in the face of enemy attacks. Later, we will take a closer look at how I believe the spirit of witchcraft attacked Bible personalities. Thank God, He always delivers from enemy oppression those who turn to Him.

Witchcraft can attack our minds and bodies through words—our own as well as others'. This means that words are not just sounds or vibrations. Jesus said that His spoken words were "spirit and . . . life" (John 6:63). Because we are spirit beings created in the image of God, I believe this applies to our words as well. Proverbs 18:21 says that death and life are in the power of the tongue. This means that the words we speak over our own lives, as well as words others speak over us, carry death or life. The force of witchcraft promotes death.

The Message translation says it like this: "Words kill, words give life; they're either poison or fruit—you choose" (Proverbs 18:21). We should choose carefully the words we speak, but we do not have any control over what other people say to us or about us. Have you ever noticed the "yuck" you feel when someone attacks you verbally? Even if you give no credence to the verbal bombs—even if you know the accusations or angry tones are untrue and undeserved—those words are containers of poisonous power, and they can affect you.

The enemy can introduce "vain imaginations" into your mind through the words of others or your own negative words spoken about yourself. Either way, the effects of spiritual witchcraft are real. These vain imaginations are thoughts and ideas contrary to the Word of God. Paul speaks of this battle in the mind in 2 Corinthians:

For though we walk in the flesh, we do not war according to the flesh. For the weapons of our warfare are not carnal but mighty in God for pulling down strongholds, casting down arguments and every high thing that exalts itself against the knowledge of God, bringing every thought into captivity, to the obedience of Christ.

2 Corinthians 10:3–5

I mentioned above that the victims of witchcraft often feel tired, oppressed or depressed. That is just how I felt out on the mission field in the stifling heat with little rest and plenty of wrong thoughts.

The Enemy Closes In

Witchcraft was attacking from all sides. I theorize that witchcraft is one of the powers listed in Ephesians 6:11–12. This power can work in the actual atmosphere, having impact on the spiritual climate over a city or region—or your home. Have you ever noticed how in some cities you feel as though the heavens are as hard as bronze? That could be due to any number of principalities and powers exerting their force on the territory. In some cases, I believe witchcraft is behind a metallic-seeming atmosphere.

In regions where witchcraft's influence is extremely heavy, sometimes my eyes begin to burn as if I am in a smoke-filled room. I cannot see the haze, but I can feel it. When I "get hit with witchcraft," as we say in spiritual warfare circles, I might also become confused, forgetful, irritable or tired. The imaginations that rage against the mind can be intense, especially if you are not quick to cast them down and choose to believe the Word of God instead. Thankfully, I now understand how to "break off" the witchcraft. But during that first mission trip I was still green—and the devil took full advantage.

For starters, the heavens were hard. Added to that, my eyes were burning. My stomach was in knots from the unusual food. My back hurt. I was weary from well-doing. I was exhausted physically. But I was thirty minutes away from finishing my race, and I did not want to give up.

Now, I had felt like giving up after the second day! But the mission leader assured us that we should never give up and never give in—that we should finish what we start, no matter what. I took those words to heart, quite literally, and, while simmering under the "injustice" of my labors, pressed through the pain—and the spiritual warfare—for the duration of the trip.

The end was finally in sight. All I had to do was document a few testimonies, and I would have the satisfaction of knowing the enemy could not stop me. This was my first major battle, and I was determined to win it. I felt that if I let the devil stop me on this assignment, my failure would haunt me. I believed that if I gave up and gave in—despite my knotted stomach and aching muscles—the devil would use that against me. I was determined to overcome in the name of Jesus!

Sidelined by the Trio

Then it happened. A fellow missionary, who had offered me much unwanted advice about how to do my assignment, and who had suggested too frequently that he should take over, informed the leadership team that I was not able to continue. He told them I was in pain. He volunteered to finish the assignment.

The words this individual spoke, which I believe were based on his desire for personal gain, released witchcraft over my already overloaded mind and body. Since words are spirit, they hit me with the impact of death.

Out of genuine concern, the mission leader told me to let my teammate take over. At this point, I had about fifteen minutes left to the finish line. I explained that I was able and wanted to finish. But the mission leader—the same one who had made clear at the outset that we must *always* finish what we start—insisted that I sit down because I looked as though I was hurting.

The directive to "sit down" knocked the wind out of me. It meant the end of my genuine desire to serve. It meant quitting when I had been coached to finish. And it meant that my sense of injustice was further outraged by my teammate's usurping my assignment. I immediately became sick to my stomach and walked quickly to the restroom, embarrassed and defeated.

I was not in there long before the final attack from the deadly trio came my way—again, through the mouth of a believer. This woman, influenced by a controlling Jezebel spirit, waited for me to emerge from the bathroom stall, and then, with an angry tone, asked, "What do you think you're doing? You are out of order! You are embarrassing our ministry leader with your tantrum!"

I was taken aback. This was not a tantrum; this was a bathroom emergency!

When I emerged from the restroom, thank God a more mature, discerning believer gently laid a hand on my shoulder and spoke a simple prayer and words of life. But, honestly, I was left battling imaginations in my mind for days. It took years for me to understand the dynamics of how witchcraft (the man's words of death) tag-teamed with the spirits of religion (my sense of overwork and injustice) and Jezebel (the woman's condemning words) to destroy my confidence and effectiveness on my first mission trip.

One of Jezebel's goals was to keep me from returning to the mission field—and it worked through religion while using witchcraft as a weapon. Of course, the strategy failed. I went back again and again and again. Many souls were saved. Many were delivered. Many were equipped. Praise God!

Jezebel and Her Witchcrafts

The Bible makes the connection between Jezebel and her witchcrafts. Second Kings tells us of a confrontation between Joram, who was a son of Queen Jezebel and Israel's reigning king, and Jehu, a military commander in Israel. God had chosen Jehu to replace Joram as king and obliterate the house of Jezebel.

When Jehu approached King Joram on this mission, the suspicious king asked if Jehu was coming in peace. Jehu replied, "What peace, so long as the harlotries of your mother Jezebel and her witchcrafts are so many?" (2 Kings 9:22 NASB). Queen Jezebel was a spiritual harlot well versed in witchcraft—divinations and enchantments—and religion. (We will discuss a "Jehu anointing" against Jezebel in chapter 4.)

Indeed, this idolatrous queen took Israel to new heights of evil by seducing her husband, King Ahab, into embracing her idolatry. Idol worship provoked the Lord to anger—and still does. (Mind you, idol worship in Christianity today typically takes on a different form. We idolize wealth, status, our bodies, sports and so on.)

Some years before this encounter between Joram and Jehu, the prophet Samuel offered keen revelation about the connection between rebellion against God and witchcraft. When rebuking King Saul for his disobedience to one of God's commands, Samuel said, "Rebellion is as the sin of witchcraft, and stubbornness is as iniquity and idolatry. Because you have rejected the word of the LORD, He also has rejected you from being king" (1 Samuel 15:23).

The hallmarks of spiritual witchcraft are rebellion and stubbornness. If you are exhibiting these behaviors, you are effectively serving the idol of self and opening yourself to spiritual witchcraft.

Witchcraft and Religion Unite

Jezebel's witchcraft often finds expression through sorcery. The word *sorcery* comes from the Hebrew word *magic*. *Magic* means "to whisper a spell." Today we call these "word curses." This is why negative, intimidating, judgmental, critical or otherwise unkind words can carry the power of death. We see clear examples of this in Scripture. The spirit of Jezebel uses people—often those with religious mindsets—to release witchcraft against us.

There is no mistaking one of the word curses that Queen Jezebel released against the great prophet Elijah. Elijah had just defeated and slain hundreds of the queen's false prophets at Mount Carmel. When Jezebel learned of this, she sent a messenger to him with these words: "So let the gods do to me, and more also, if I do not make your life as the life of one of them by tomorrow about this time" (1 Kings 19:2).

The result: Elijah was covered in witchcraft, which released imaginations against his mind. The next verse says that "when he *saw* that, he arose and ran for his life, and went to Beer-sheba, which belongs to Judah, and left his servant there" (1 Kings 19:3, emphasis added). I believe that Elijah, being a prophet, saw a fearful vision in his mind and ran after he heard the words of Jezebel's messenger. He saw a picture of the outcome Jezebel was threatening.

Where does the spirit of religion fit into this mix? Consider how Elijah defeated Jezebel's pagan religion on the showdown at Mount Carmel. Jezebel had 850 false prophets on her payroll—400 prophets of Baal and 450 prophets of Asherah. Elijah told King Ahab to gather all Israel and the 850 false prophets on Mount Carmel for a showdown. "And Elijah came to all the people, and said, 'How long will you falter between two opinions? If the LORD is God, follow Him; but if Baal, follow him.' But the people answered him not a word" (1 Kings 18:21).

After the false prophets failed to prove their god was alive, Elijah repaired the altar of the Lord and went on to prove by fire who the real God was—Jehovah. Elijah effectively exposed Jezebel's false religion. The Israelites acknowledged the true God, seized the prophets of Baal and executed them at Elijah's order (see 1 Kings 18:40). Shortly thereafter, Jezebel released witchcraft via a word curse against Elijah. He ran for his life. And soon enough the religious spirit went to work on his mind.

Religion's Self-Righteousness

Let's take another moment to connect the spirit of religion to Elijah's story so you can see how Jezebel uses it in partnership with witchcraft. Once we connect these dots, we can begin to build on this revelation and expose the attack against you by this unholy trinity in greater detail.

The spirit of religion wields a double-edged sword through legalism and self-righteousness. On one edge of the blade, legalism offers rules and regulations that supposedly justify you in God's eyes. The only problem is, of course, keeping rules and regulations is not what justifies you in God's eyes. Faith in Jesus Christ is. While we should set our hearts to obey God's commands, we do not find our righteousness in rules. We find our righteousness in the work of the cross and our trust in the God who did the work.

The other edge, self-righteousness, results when you are convinced you have met legalism's rules and regulations—and especially when you see that others have not performed to your standards. Once the spirit of witchcraft was at work against him, Elijah gave in to the imaginations and expressed self-righteousness. Twice he told the Lord, "I have been very zealous for the LORD God of hosts; for the children of Israel have forsaken Your covenant, torn down Your altars, and killed Your prophets with the sword. I alone am left; and they seek to take my life" (1 Kings 19:10; see also verse 14).

The children of Israel had just made a clear choice for Jehovah by seizing the prophets of Baal and executing them. Yes, Israel had turned to idols in Jezebel's kingdom, but once they had seen a sign from the God who answers by fire, the Israelites had submitted to Elijah's orders. Elijah seemed to have forgotten all about that and set himself apart as superior to the children of Israel.

Influenced by the spirit of religion and exhibiting self-righteousness, Elijah reminded God of Israel's past sins and puffed himself up. And that is part of religion's warfare strategy: It uses self-righteousness to keep you wallowing in condemnation over your failure or to puff you up into spiritual pride over your accomplishments.

Still, we need to give Elijah grace upon grace—after all, he made those statements after enduring a battle of biblical proportions with Jezebel, witchcraft and 850 false prophets, and the spirit of religion had already been working on him.

How do we know it had been working on him? Because he had made a similar statement to the Israelites at Mount Carmel before the battle had ever begun and before Jezebel's direct witchcraft curse had been released in his hearing. Specifically, Elijah had said, "I alone am left a prophet of the LORD" (1 Kings 18:22). That was his mindset—it was not the truth. He had not had prophetic revelation on the matter. He was wrong. I believe it was the religious spirit working on him even then.

Elijah was hardly the only one who remained loyal to God, but the spirit of religion had convinced him otherwise. Yet the Lord did not correct Elijah's presumptuous religious thinking until after the battle with the false prophets. When Elijah complained to the Lord twice that he was the only one left to stand up for God's honor, God told the prophet, "I have reserved seven thousand in Israel, all whose knees have not bowed to Baal, and every mouth that has not kissed him" (1 Kings 19:18). Our gentle God did not rebuke Elijah for his wrong thinking, but nevertheless set the record straight.

I mentioned that self-righteousness can keep us wallowing in condemnation. If we fail to live up to the standard that self-righteousness establishes, religion cuts us down. Religious condemnation cannot strip us of the righteousness we have in Christ, but it is part of religion's agenda. We will talk more about that in a later chapter.

For now, I trust you can see that the spirits of Jezebel, religion and witchcraft do not work in silos. In other words, they are not isolated one from another. Satan's army is highly organized. I believe demons plot and plan together for our destruction. Where you find one member of this deadly trio you will usually find another—and often all three. As you read the pages of this book, I pray that the Holy Spirit will reveal to you the shrewd strategies by which these wicked spirits work together.

2

Jezebel's Idolatrous Agenda

Growing up, I had a collection of rock star idols. I clipped their glam shots out of *Tiger Beat* and taped them to my wall. I spent every spare penny I had (even skipping lunch) on their music, T shirts, buttons and stickers—and I camped out overnight in all kinds of weather with like-minded groupies hoping to get a good seat at their concerts. Talk about devotion!

It turns out, this same devotion can be found in the church. But it is not always to Jesus. Sometimes it is to various false gods—from money, to physical beauty, to power, to success, to, yes, even charismatic preachers who spin gospels of entitlement that encourage us to pursue the idols we covet.

Jezebel has escorted many believers to the altars of idols—false gods that relegate Jesus to something less than first place in our lives. And Jezebel has done this, ironically, in the name of religion.

Yes, Jezebel and religion are in cahoots to woo us from our first love. We may indeed perform plenty of good religious works while we chase our idols—but that does not make up for putting Jesus second (or third or fourth) in our hearts. Here is one common strategy you might have run into: Jezebel, who teaches false doctrines of grace that give you a license to sin (see Revelation 2:20), tells you that Jesus understands you are too busy serving in His Kingdom to make a heart connection with Him. Meanwhile, the spirit of religion affirms your worth based on good works rather than justification by faith (see Ephesians 2:8–9). The ultimate deception is that our religious works justify our pursuit of idols in the name of Jesus.

Can you see it? We need to learn to discern this one-two punch from Jezebel and religion and repent, because like the church at Ephesus, when we take this idolatrous path away from God in the name of God, Jesus has something against us. He still loves us with a passion, of course, but He nevertheless has something against us. Consider Jesus' warning to the church at Ephesus:

> "I know your works, your labor, your patience, and that you cannot bear those who are evil. And you have tested those who say they are apostles and are not, and have found them liars; and you have persevered and have patience, and have labored for My name's sake and have not become weary. Nevertheless I have this against you, that you have left your first love. Remember therefore from where you have fallen; repent and do the first works."
>
> Revelation 2:2–5

Think about it for a minute. This Ephesian revival center was doing plenty of good works and discerning false apostles. It sounds like a safe place to worship. But the spirit of religion crept in and those good works became a backdrop for idolatry. It is easy enough to fall into the trap of religious performance and become more fervent about the work of the ministry than the God of the ministry.

Here is the secret of balancing devotion to Jesus and works in His name: We must keep "the first works"—the heart of devotion and zeal we experienced when we were saved—and allow our ministry works to flow out of that love for God rather than our pursuit of recognition, prosperity or success.

If we fail to do this, we could end up like Ahab.

Rock Star Ahab

King Ahab was akin to a rock star in his day. He was a strong warrior who saw two major victories in battles with the Syrians (see 1 Kings 20). He was famous and wealthy; he built an ivory house for himself (see 1 Kings 22:39). The last king before him to post so many victories was none other than Solomon. But for all his recorded success, the Bible says Ahab was evil in the Lord's sight—even more than all of the kings who came before him (see 1 Kings 16:30). That says a lot, considering how evil some of Ahab's predecessors were.

Ahab did more to provoke the anger of the Lord than any other king up to his reign (see 1 Kings 16:33). What exactly did Ahab do? He mixed politics with religion in an alliance with Ethbaal, the king of the Sidonians. As part of that political alliance, Ahab married Ethbaal's daughter, Jezebel, who seduced him deeply into idolatry—and it did not take long. When we align ourselves with people or make alliances apart from the Spirit's leading, we can be turned away from our first love to the idolatry of success, power, money—or just about anything other than Jesus.

After Ahab united with Jezebel, he quickly adopted Jezebel's religion, which included witchcraft and harlotries (see 2 Kings 9:22). Watch how fast the coalition of religion, witchcraft and Jezebel happens: Ahab "took as wife Jezebel the daughter of Ethbaal, king of the Sidonians; and he went and served Baal and worshiped him. Then he set up an altar for Baal in the temple of Baal, which he had built in Samaria. And Ahab made a wooden image" (1 Kings 16:31–33). Yes, he forsook Jehovah and started worshiping the gods of the Sidonians just that fast.

Ahab knew better. God had spoken clearly against idol worship when He commanded, "You shall have no other gods before Me. You shall not make for yourself a carved image, or any likeness of anything that is in heaven above, or that is in the earth beneath, or that is in the water under the earth; you shall not bow down to them nor serve them" (Exodus 20:3–5).

Jonah learned the hard way, sitting in the belly of a whale, that rebellion is as the sin of witchcraft (see 1 Samuel 15:23). He discovered that "those who regard worthless idols forsake their own mercy" (Jonah 2:8). David warned, "Their sorrows shall be multiplied who hasten after another god" (Psalm 16:4). But somehow Jezebel, perhaps using her witchcrafts, was able to woo Ahab into the cesspool of idolatry.

With idolatry reaching unprecedented heights in Israel, Jezebel set out to cut off the true prophetic voices in the land that could speak against her witchcrafts and harlotries: Jezebel massacred the Lord's prophets. Obadiah, who was in charge of Ahab's house, took one hundred prophets and hid them, fifty each in two caves, and fed them bread and water (see 1 Kings 18:3–4). Jezebel is still working to silence the voices of true prophets who identify defiled religion and witchcraft. But Jezebel would rather make us one of its idolatrous puppets. We will look more closely at Jezebel's puppets in the next chapter.

The writers of the New Testament understood the danger of idolatry all too well. John warns us to "keep yourselves from idols" (1 John 5:21), and Paul warns us to "flee from idolatry" (1 Corinthians 10:14). Idolaters will not inherit the Kingdom of God (see 1 Corinthians 6:9). Jezebel knows that. Ahab went headlong into disaster, being killed in battle after receiving a false prophecy from four hundred of Jezebel's prophetic puppets, who agreed he should wage war to take the city of Ramoth Gilead out of the hands of his enemies. Ahab had a true witness from an uncompromising prophet named Micaiah, but he decided to put God's prophet in prison and follow the counsel of the idolatrous false prophets (see 1 Kings 22).

The deadly trio—Jezebel's idolatry, the spirit of religion and his own witchcraft evident in rebellion—led to Ahab's death, and his kingdom came crashing down. The same thing is happening in many churches today: Idolatry—which is exhibited through things like power, sex and money—is often at the root of church scandals. Jezebel, working through religion, plants the seeds of idolatry into the souls of leaders, who then fall into greed and immorality.

How Jezebel and Religion Prop Up Pastors

Encouraging idolatry is a characteristic Jezebel and religion share. Jezebel and religion tag-team to position pastors, whether in the local pulpit, on television or online, as idols so the trusting sheep will let their guard down. Immature, naïve, lukewarm or lazy believers begin to buy in to what their religious idols preach, rarely opening the Bible to compare what they are hearing with the truth of God's Word. That makes them easy prey to buy in to something else: deception and merchandising schemes. We will look more closely at that in a minute.

The apostle Paul warned believers about making idols out of spiritual leaders (see 1 Corinthians 1:10–15). Idolizing spiritual leaders can lead to disunity, religious pride and deception of all kinds. There is certainly nothing wrong with admiring a minister for being dedicated to the Lord, to His work and to His people. But when we idolize someone, it creates a false image and generates a perception that the revered one can do no wrong. This is one reason why people are so devastated when leaders fall. Sure, it is hurtful at any level. But when believers put more faith in the pastor than they put in Jesus—and then that pastor falls—their faith is shaken to the core because their faith was in the wrong place.

So, again, the spirit of religion works to make idols out of ministers. In other words, the spirit of religion influences well-meaning believers to puff up Christian personalities like rock stars.

On the other side of the pulpit (or the TV screen) Jezebel looks for greed in the pastor's heart and sets out to help him get what he wants, just as Queen Jezebel saw the greed in Ahab's heart and set out to help him get Naboth's vineyard. The greed-inspired pastor hands his authority over to Jezebel, and because religion has set him up as an idol, he begins merchandising the Gospel.

When preachers begin to merchandise the Gospel— promising prophecies, anointing or generalized breakthroughs if you sow a special (financial) seed into their ministries—they are tapping in to the Jezebel spirit.

Peter exposed this:

But there were also false prophets among the people, even as there will be false teachers among you, who will secretly bring in destructive heresies, even denying the Lord who bought them, and bring on themselves swift destruction. And many will follow their destructive ways, because of whom the way of truth will be blasphemed. By covetousness they will exploit you with deceptive words; for a long time their judgment has not been idle, and their destruction does not slumber.

2 Peter 2:1–3

Indeed, Jesus rebuked the church at Thyatira—a church known for its works, love, service, faith and patience—for allowing a woman flowing in a Jezebel spirit to teach and seduce believers in to idolatry and sexual immorality (see Revelation 2:20). By *flowing in* I mean tapping into or being influenced by a particular spiritual influence, whether good or evil. Jezebel wants to seduce you away from God. She wants you to worship her idols—and she wants to murder you if you will not submit. That is why believers who expose problems like idolatry or immorality or other sins in the church become the problem.

Beyond the merchandising preachers, there is a deeper, more dangerous strategy of religion and Jezebel: the idolatrous gospel.

Jezebel's Idolatrous Gospel

Jezebel introduced an idolatrous gospel to Israel that was deadly. In partnership with the spirit of religion, Jezebel is still using the same strategy today. Sadly, the Western church has made rock stars out of many preachers. In other words, there are preachers in mega-churches and small storefront churches alike who are idolized by their congregations. The pastor has seemingly taken the place of Jesus in their lives.

Rather than running to the throne, they run to the pastor. And rather than running to the Word for truth, they take everything the pastor says as gospel (whether it is true or not). Idolizing preachers is never appropriate—but it can be especially dangerous if those preachers are not aligning themselves with the Word of God. If preachers do not stay humble and point people to Jesus—if they tap in to the adoration from their followers—they end up preaching messages that tickle people's ears rather than bring heart-changing Holy Ghost conviction to their souls. Some preachers, in fact, are presenting a hyped-up, watered-down, seeker-friendly gospel that is giving the assurance of heaven while leaving the congregants in prime position for hell.

I am convinced that many people who claim to be Christ's followers are not really saved, because false teachers and false prophets are propagating among them a "different gospel" centered on "another Jesus" (2 Corinthians 11:3–4). I am also convinced that many self-professing saints are going to sit right next to sinners in hell when it is all said and done—thanks, in part, to rock-star preachers presenting a hyped-up, watered-down, seeker-friendly gospel centered on idolatry. When you pull back the mask, you find Jezebel and religion smirking at the idolaters in their Sunday best.

Especially in America, it is easy to say, "I believe in Jesus." It is called mental assent. I believed in Jesus before I got saved, too, but I was still on my way to hell. Too many who have "accepted Jesus into their hearts" have responded to a "different gospel" centered on a false Christ.

What do these gospels espouse? These gospels are mixed with compromise. They are impure and defiled religion. They offer a humanistic, self-help message that taps in to New Age principles. Indeed, these false teachers and false prophets are moving in a false anointing and presenting a false Christ. And it is deadly.

Perverting the Gospel of Christ

Jesus exposed Jezebel's agenda to "teach and seduce [His] servants to commit sexual immorality and eat things sacrificed to idols" (Revelation 2:20). In other words, Jezebel propagates a doctrine of false grace and excuses our spiritual adultery and idolatry.

This is not a new problem. Look again at Paul's words, written two thousand years ago:

> But I fear, lest somehow, as the serpent deceived Eve by his craftiness, so your minds may be corrupted from the simplicity that is in Christ. For if he who comes preaches *another Jesus* whom we have not preached, or if you receive a different spirit which you have not received, or a *different gospel* which you have not accepted—you may well put up with it!
>
> 2 Corinthians 11:3–4, emphasis added

The Gospel is not difficult to understand, and it is not difficult to recognize false doctrine if you are a student of the Word. But too many people do not open their Bibles and read Scripture for themselves. Too many prefer a twenty-minute sermonette rather than a challenge to die to self, pick up their crosses and walk the narrow road. They have turned away from the real Jesus to another Jesus. Paul felt angst in his spirit over this.

> I marvel that you are turning away so soon from Him who called you in the grace of Christ, to a *different gospel*, which is not another; but there are some who trouble you and want to pervert the gospel of Christ. But even if we, or an angel

from heaven, preach any other gospel to you than what we have preached to you, let him be accursed. As we have said before, so now I say again, if anyone preaches any other gospel to you than what you have received, let him be accursed.

Galatians 1:6–9, emphasis added

What are these gospels? Some that we hear today espouse *universalism*: There is no hell; we are all going to heaven in the end. Some propose *hyper-grace*: We have license to sin; Jesus has already paid the penalty. Some rely on *humanism*: We are ourselves gods; our lives are our own. False teachers might start with Scripture to justify their positions, but they wind up twisting truth into fables and fairy tales.

The Get-Rich-Quick Gospel

Beyond universalism, hyper-grace and humanism, one of the most dangerous false gospels that religion and Jezebel propagate is the *get-rich-quick gospel*. It is also called the prosperity gospel.

You may remember the question-mark-suit-wearing Matthew Lesko, the infomercial icon who peddled many books, including *Free Money to Pay Your Bills*. The New York State Consumer Protection Board exposed him for misleading advertisements, but not before he sold countless books at forty dollars a pop that he admittedly plagiarized. Get-rich-quick-gospel gainsayers are a little more difficult to expose but not hard to discern.

Then there was the "Greatest Vitamin in the World" heist of Don Lapre. All you had to do was send him $35 for a chance to make millions selling vitamins, which promised to help with everything from diabetes to cancer. There is no telling how much Lapre raked in before the Food and Drug

Administration warned the public about his false advertising. Likewise, there is no telling how much the get-rich-quick-gospel preachers will stuff into their pockets before truth catches up with them.

It seems that even Spirit-filled, blood-bought believers are buying in to the most outlandish scams in order to make miracle money. Some of these are worldly scams; others are churchly scams. Both are leaving believers with big promises and dented bank accounts, and both show desperation or lack of discernment—or both—among many in the Body of Christ.

A pastor friend of mine told me about a member of his church whose bank account was completely wiped out because he fell for the "Spanish prisoner" scam. You may know it as the "Nigerian 419" scam. You get an email from Nigeria (or India or Russia or South Africa) asking you to help the sender access unclaimed money in exchange for a cut of a multimillion-dollar inheritance. Scammers ask you to wire money to pay costs associated with processing the claim.

This poor gullible saint praised the Lord when he received the email offer. He had been praying for a financial breakthrough and saw the opportunity as a miracle answer from God! My pastor friend—and others—warned him that it was what the old-timers called a "confidence trick," but he was either too desperate or too naive to heed the wisdom. He sowed thousands of dollars because he was utterly convinced he would soon be a multimillionaire. His lack of discernment—and his refusal to take wise counsel—devastated his finances.

Recognizing Merchandising Gospels

The get-rich-quick gospel often works in the same way. You get email from a ministry asking for your help to keep a television broadcast on the air—or maybe keep an orphanage open in Nigeria. There is nothing wrong with ministries sending out pleas for donations. The problem is what some of these ministries are promising in return. The get-rich-quick-gospel scams make shallow promises that are not likely to come true for anyone—except for the few who are propagating the message. Let's look at a couple of these gimmicks.

Maybe you have watched Christian television programs—or even seen in person—saints coming and laying money at the feet of the preacher, leaving it on the stage or even stuffing it in his pockets as he walks by. The idea here is to give money during a time of anointing in order to get a quick return. People are sowing into the message they hear in order to reap a harvest.

Scripturally, they stand on Acts 4:34–35, but they blur the context: "Nor was there anyone among them who lacked; for all who were possessors of lands or houses sold them, and brought the proceeds of the things that were sold, and laid them at the apostles' feet; and they distributed to each as anyone had need." This verse speaks of distributing goods for the needs of people in the early Church—not heaping up a quick financial return on a seed offering because of a "special anointing" on a message.

Or maybe you have seen variations of other swindles using Scripture, such as those who use Luke 6:38: "Give, and it will be given to you: good measure, pressed down, shaken together, and running over will be put into your bosom. For with the same measure that you use, it will be measured back to you." The preacher says he had a vision or received a prophetic word that all those who commit to sowing $638 over the next six months will get a massive financial breakthrough. Other gospel hucksters have offered a $1,000 return on a $58 seed—but only if you will quickly go to the phone right now! And you had better hurry because it is available for only three hundred people who really need a miracle.

Others just look for pledges to give in exchange for anointed prayer, but later harass you with letters reminding you to keep your vow. Still others offer special anointed prayer shawls, anointing oil, special soaps or other merchandise that promises miracles in exchange for big bucks.

Usually it does not take much discernment to recognize one of these schemes, but they are not always so blatant. Sometimes it is much more subtle. That is why you need to stop and pray about your giving. If you sow a seed into a false prophet's pot looking for a quick prayer answer, you are not likely to get the reward you are looking for. As with the local pastor who fell for the Nigerian scam, the miracle is not likely to manifest.

Worldly get-rich-quick schemes and churchly get-rich-quick schemes have plenty in common. Typically, both imply a fast return on your investment thanks to a special revelation or a special anointing. Both also use pressure tactics to get you to let go of your cash quickly before you have time to consider what you are doing. Sometimes they use testimonies from others who previously bought in to the message and found fast success.

Do not fall for these tactics in the world or in the church. Again, the only ones getting rich off get-rich-quick schemes are the ones crafting the scams—or helping promote the scams. Yes, they will have to answer to God one day for fleecing the sheep. But that does not mean you have no responsibility to be a discerning, wise steward.

So, believe God wants to prosper you, but never buy in to the get-rich-quick gospel. It does not work any better than Lesko's "Free Money to Pay Your Bills" scam. And Jezebel laughs all the way to the bank.

Escaping Jezebel's Idolatrous Clutches

If you are reading this book, then you have probably already chosen this day whom you will serve. But could it be possible that there are yet things you need to put away in order to worship the Lord in spirit and in truth, and to love Him with all your heart, with all your soul, with all your strength and with all your mind? I submit to you that it is possible, and for many of us even probable.

Today, the Lord is calling you to the Valley of Shechem. Here is where you can, by your will, shake free from Jezebel's idolatry.

Until recently, I had not spent much time studying the rich biblical history of the Valley of Shechem, the place where Abraham first built an altar to the Lord on his migration out of an idolatrous land. I had never done an intense analysis of this valley between mounts Ebal and Gerizim, where Jacob built his well and where Jesus would later tell a woman everything she had ever done (see Joshua 8:33; John 4).

No, I did not know much about this significant valley. It took only three words from the Lord to pique my curiosity. He said to me, *Valley of Shechem.* Those three words set me off on a prophetic investigation of what the Lord is saying to the Church in this hour. I studied the geographical and historical significance of Shechem, but it is the spiritual significance on which the Lord shone a bright light.

The Valley of Shechem is where Joshua called together all the tribes of Israel to make a covenant. Once all the elders, chiefs, judges and officers arrived and presented themselves before God, Joshua delivered a powerful prophetic word to the nations. Joshua reminded the people how God had called Abraham "from the other side of the River," where Israel's ancestors had served other gods (Joshua 24:2). He talked about the plagues on Egypt, and the parting of the Red Sea. He essentially offered a history of Israel right up to its modern day. God was reminding them of the kind intentions of His will.

God was going somewhere with this prophetic history lesson. Indeed, He was working methodically to drive home a point. See, God had given Israel a land for which she had not labored and cities she had not built. Israel was dwelling safely in her Promised Land, eating from the vineyards and the olive groves provided there. In other words, God followed His miraculous deliverance with His abundant grace. Much the same, God

> has blessed us with every spiritual blessing in heavenly places in Christ, just as He chose us in Him before the foundation of the world, that we should be holy and without blame before Him in love, having predestined us to adoption as sons by Jesus Christ to Himself, according to the good pleasure of His will, to the praise of the glory of His grace, by which He made us accepted in the Beloved.
>
> Ephesians 1:3–6

With this spiritual truth in mind, come with me to the Valley of Shechem and listen closely to the heart of the prophetic message Joshua delivered to Israel on that day of decision—then apply it to yourself.

> "Now therefore, fear the LORD, serve Him in sincerity and in truth, and put away the gods which your fathers served on the other side of the River and in Egypt. Serve the LORD! And if it seems evil to you to serve the LORD, choose for yourselves this day whom you will serve, whether the gods which your fathers served that were on the other side of the River, or the

gods of the Amorites, in whose land you dwell. But as for me and my house, we will serve the LORD."

Joshua 24:14–15

The question is simple: Will you serve Jehovah whole-heartedly or will you serve an idol? The simplest definition of *idol* is "a false god." Merriam-Webster defines *idol* as "a representation or symbol of an object of worship." Another definition is "pretender, impostor." Still another definition is "an object of extreme devotion" or "a false conception."

In ancient times, people created idols to worship. They gave these wooden, silver and golden idols names that represented gods. Today, we are a little more sophisticated, and the enemy is a little subtler. We would never dream of worshiping a golden calf. But we might be tempted to worship our favorite sports, our careers, our children or even our ministries. In other words, we might set up people, places and things as idols in our lives that draw our attention away from God. Anything that draws our attention away from Jesus is a pretender and an imposter. Any object of extreme devotion apart from God is a false god.

The Bible clearly says, "You shall have no other gods before me" (Exodus 20:3). In case we did not hear it loud and clear in Exodus, the Holy Spirit repeats Himself in Deuteronomy 5:7: "You shall have no other gods before me." And once more, "You shall worship no other god, for the LORD, whose name is Jealous, is a jealous God" (Exodus 34:14).

Maybe you have "idols" in your life, like your kids or your car. This is what the Lord is saying in this hour: More often than not the idol in our lives is *self*.

The Bible says that stubbornness is the same as idolatry (1 Samuel 15:23). Stubbornness is putting self-will before God's will. The Lord is saying that now is the time for our self-will to decrease so that His will can increase in the earth. Now is the time for us to lay aside childish ways and adopt His ways for His glory. Now is the time for us to surrender with all our hearts, with all our souls, with all our strength to the will of God—even at the expense of our personal ambitions, hopes and plans. It is time to lay everything on the altar and let the Lord give back only that which agrees with His plans and purposes.

Jesus told the woman at the well in the Valley of Shechem that God is Spirit, and His worshipers must worship in spirit and in truth. So choose this day whom you will serve: self or Spirit.

I urge you by the Spirit of God and in the words of Scripture not to be conformed to this world, but to be transformed by the renewing of your mind, that you may prove what is that good and acceptable and perfect will of God to a lost and dying world. And I pray that you may be filled with the knowledge of His will in all wisdom and spiritual understanding—and that you may be strengthened with all might, according to His glorious power to obey the will of God in all things.

When you do, it is tough for Jezebel and her spirit of religion to move you from the Rock on which you stand. Amen.

3

Identifying Jezebel's Puppets

Maggie was the most faithful servant in the congregation.
Single and in her forties, she was the first one to arrive at
church and the last one to leave. Eventually, Pastor Jake appointed her to the ministry of helps. Although she was self-employed, Maggie started spending more time volunteering
at the church than she did working on her entrepreneurial
ventures. She even moved her office into the church to be more
available to Pastor Jake during business hours.

It was not long before Maggie was struggling to pay her
bills. Despite advice from close friends to pull back from so
much volunteer work, she pressed into her role as minister of
helps. Misguided prophets in the church repeatedly declared
financial increase over Maggie's life—and she stood on those
words, even while neglecting her business.

Maggie truly had a servant's heart—but she also had a
wounded heart. Her mother had abandoned the family just
days after Maggie was born, leaving a deep hurt in her soul.
She sought solace in works of service. Although she was the

youngest sibling in the family, she took on the role of problem-solver, peacemaker and, in many ways, provider. Maggie laid her life down for her family because she felt guilty that her mother had left just after she was born. She took the blame. After she accepted Jesus as her Savior and got plugged in to a church, it did not take Jezebel long to make Maggie—with all her good intentions and works of service—into a puppet. Pastor Jake was more interested in building his personal kingdom than the Kingdom of God. When he saw her heart to serve, he swiftly put her into action—calling her into a position of leadership before she was stable in the Word. With regard to appointing leadership positions in the church, the apostle Paul warned "not a novice, lest being puffed up with pride he fall into the same condemnation as the devil" (1 Timothy 3:6).

Wielding the authority she had been given by Pastor Jake, Maggie fell into the snare of pride. Theirs was a Jezebel/Ahab–type relationship: Pastor Jake under the Ahab spirit empowered Maggie to do his dirty work, as long as she served his purposes. When she fell short, Maggie was spiritually castrated by the pastor's hot anger. The rebukes caused her to work even harder to avoid his wrath and win his favor.

Maggie looked like the pastor's puppet, but she was really Jezebel and Ahab's puppet. And so was Pastor Jake. The passive-aggressive pastor was flowing in a spirit of Ahab that manifested through low self-esteem masked by pride, fear of rejection masked with a competitive spirit and temper tantrums. The pastor set himself up as an idol whom no one could question. All those who did not obey him were labeled rebellious, while those who were obedient to him were allowed to serve in ministry—even one individual who fell into immorality. The spirit of Jezebel seduces believers into idolatry and immorality (see Revelation 2:20). Ahab allows it. Maggie became a eunuch to Jezebel and Ahab.

Jezebel is savvy—and does not work alone. Remember, Queen Jezebel was devout in her religion and the false prophetess Jezebel in the book of Revelation was actually teaching in the church! Jesus condemned the church of Thyatira for allowing that spirit of seduction to remain in its midst (see Revelation 2:20). Seduction is the essence of the Jezebel spirit. Again, Jezebel seeks to seduce the saints into idolatry and sexual immorality. The Bible records the names of some people Queen Jezebel seduced successfully. I call them Jezebel's puppets: King Ahab, the 850 false prophets she kept under her thumb and the eunuchs she used to do her bidding.

Queen Jezebel worked through the spirit of religion to seduce those around her into worshiping false gods—effectively cutting them off from the living God and bringing His judgment (through famine) on the land. Jezebel is most effective working through governments (weakened Ahabs), church systems (false prophets) and deceived believers (servile eunuchs). In this chapter, we will take a closer look at these puppets.

Jezebel Seduces Ahab

King Ahab seemed hell-bent on provoking God from the moment he took the throne. His first recorded move, as we noted earlier, was to marry Sidonian King Ethbaal's daughter Jezebel and serve her gods (see 1 Kings 16:31). We noted also that Ahab did more to provoke God to anger than any other king before him (see 1 Kings 16:33). What was Ahab's great sin? Ahab broke not only the first Commandment by worshiping Baal, but also the second Commandment by building a temple and an altar for Baal in Samaria, as well as an Asherah pole to please Jezebel (see 1 Kings 16:32–33).

Ahab was one of Jezebel's puppets, submitting to her willfully. Like the puppeteer she is, Jezebel manipulated Ahab through his lusts and emotions. Ahab wore the king's signet ring and sat on the throne, but Jezebel was working with the spirit of religion to pull his strings. The spirit of religion has a form of godliness, but denies its power (see 2 Timothy 3:5). In other words, Baal worship made a show of religion—but was powerless and adulterous. Jezebel's religion led Ahab into idolatry, immorality and all forms of wickedness.

Ahab stood by as Jezebel massacred the prophets of the Lord (see 1 Kings 18:4). It was not as if Ahab was an Old Testament New Ager who worshiped this, that and the other god. Ahab made his choice of gods clear when he did nothing to protect Jehovah's true prophets; nor did he reprove Jezebel for massacring them. Jezebel persecuted God's followers. She wanted to murder anyone who pledged allegiance to God and God alone. And she used her position in Ahab's kingdom to execute her will.

Ahab was loyal to Jezebel and Jezebel alone. When Elijah defeated the 850 false prophets at the Mount Carmel showdown, Ahab ran back and told Jezebel, and she plotted a murder against yet another prophet (see 1 Kings 19:1–2). Ahab also provided for Jezebel's prophets to live in luxury. These men were on the state payroll and lived the high life—all in exchange for telling Jezebel what she wanted to hear.

Ahab realized certain benefits, of course, by allowing Jezebel to usurp his kingship. Indeed, Jezebel gave him what he wanted to placate his lusts. We mentioned Naboth earlier. Jezebel had this innocent man condemned and murdered so a depressed Ahab could claim his vineyard (see 1 Kings 21). Ultimately, serving Jezebel and her gods instead of the God of Israel—becoming by his own free will one of Jezebel's puppets—cost Ahab not only his own life, but his whole house (see 2 Kings 9:7–8).

The Bible says, "There was no one like Ahab who sold himself to do wickedness in the sight of the LORD, because Jezebel his wife stirred him up" (1 Kings 21:25). Even though Ahab followed Jezebel into sin, God still held him accountable. In other words, he could not say, "Jezebel made me do it!" Ahab's heart was already bent toward evil when he decided to marry her. Perhaps she incited him to worse sin than he would have pursued in his own lusts, but, in the end, each individual is still responsible for his or her own character.

It is not difficult to find various checklists regarding the characteristics Ahab exhibited; a quick check online reveals several. Most of these, however, are based on general personal experience rather than Scripture. Practical experience is helpful, but we should look to Scripture to understand how spirits—good and evil—operate. Everything else is anecdotal and not always accurate.

So before we move on to Jezebel's next puppet, let's look at some of the scriptural revelations concerning Ahab. From there, we can better discern the spirit of Ahab—but remember always to rely on the Holy Spirit in the matter of discerning spirits or you could wind up battling the wrong spirit.

Ahab Is Not a Lover of the Truth

King Ahab was a lover of Jezebel, a lover of himself, a lover of power—but he did not love the truth (see 2 Thessalonians 2:10). What is more, he made an enemy out of anyone who told him the truth or who stood for God. After God sent a famine to the land of Samaria, Ahab called Elijah a "troubler of Israel." Elijah set the record straight, telling Ahab that he was the one troubling Israel, "in that you have forsaken the commandments of the LORD and followed the Baals" (1 Kings 1:17–18).

The spirit of Ahab makes an enemy out of truth-speakers. I was once part of a church where Jezebel was reigning. The spirit of Ahab was working through the senior pastor. When I recognized and pointed out the Jezebel influence, speaking the truth in love, I was treated like "the enemy" by those under its power. We see King Ahab work this way in Scripture. After Ahab stole Naboth's vineyard, the Lord sent Elijah to deliver a message to him. "So Ahab said to Elijah, 'Have you found me, O my enemy?'" (1 Kings 21:20). And let's not forget the godly prophet Micaiah. He would not prophesy what Ahab wanted to hear, and it landed him in prison (see 1 Kings 22).

Ahab Is Covetous, Idolatrous and Rebellious

Ahab broke the first and second Commandments—"You shall have no other gods before Me" (Exodus 20:3) and "You shall not make for yourself a carved image . . . you shall not bow down to them nor serve them" (Exodus 20:4–5)—but Ahab also broke the tenth Commandment. He coveted what belonged to his neighbor. He wanted Naboth's vineyard and used Jezebel to get it for him. We know that Ahab was rebellious against the Word of God because he consistently broke the Law. And, of course, idolatry was the sin that opened the door to all the rest.

Ahab Is Emotionally Unstable

King Ahab was an emotional mess. When he did not get his way regarding the vineyard, for instance, he became sullen and angry (see 1 Kings 21:4). The king exhibited petulance and insecurity. This is why he kept the "yes-men" prophets around him, and why he allowed the strong-willed Jezebel to usurp his authority. Ultimately, Ahab catered to his emotions rather than to his spirit. He was led by the lusts of the flesh rather than the Spirit of God.

Ahab's Repentance Is False

False repentance is akin to false humility. When the Lord sent Elijah to Ahab with a word of condemnation, Ahab appeared to repent but it was false. Elijah spoke these words prophetically:

> "'Behold, I will bring calamity on you. I will take away your posterity, and will cut off from Ahab every male in Israel, both bond and free. I will make your house like the house of Jeroboam the son of Nebat, and like the house of Baasha the son of Ahijah, because of the provocation with which you have provoked Me to anger, and made Israel sin.' And concerning Jezebel the LORD also spoke, saying, 'The dogs shall eat Jezebel by the wall of Jezreel.' The dogs shall eat whoever belongs to Ahab and dies in the city, and the birds of the air shall eat whoever dies in the field."
>
> 1 Kings 21:21–24

How did Ahab respond? "He tore his clothes and put sack-cloth on his body, and fasted and lay in sackcloth, and went about mourning" (1 Kings 21:27). Although the repentance delayed God's judgment, Ahab's heart really did not change. It is like the naughty child who says he is sorry, but only because he got caught. He goes right back out and does the very same thing again.

Ahab rent his garments, but not his heart. We know this because Ahab did not forsake his idols; he did not return Naboth's vineyard to its rightful heirs; and he did not bring Jezebel into order. He then went on to put Micaiah in prison. Ultimately, actions speak louder than words. Ahab remained Jezebel's puppet until the day he died.

Jezebel's 850 Prophetic Puppets

Along with the king, Jezebel had 850 false prophetic puppets at her disposal. These prophets were actually from two different camps in Israel—the prophets of Baal and the prophets of Asherah. Queen Jezebel's false prophets were wrapped up in a religious system that spoke contrary to the will of God, while Jehovah's true prophets were hidden in caves for fear of their lives.

Ironic is the fact that Queen Jezebel was treating the true prophets of God like false prophets, while the false prophets were pampered. God had mandated that false prophets be put to death (see Deuteronomy 13:1–5) along with people who adopted idolatry or led others into this spiritual adultery (see Deuteronomy 13:12–18; 17:1–5). Jezebel had executed the true prophets of God under false pretenses to protect her puppets, so it is no wonder she was murderously mad when Elijah executed justice against them.

Who were these 850 false prophets? How did Jezebel and religion work together to fulfill their idolatrous agenda through these puppets? And how can we apply the lesson learned here to modern times? This last question is vital, as prophetic cults currently rising in the Body of Christ are deceiving and being deceived (see 2 Timothy 3:13). Should we be surprised? The Bible warns of false prophets over and over again.

Just as true prophets traveled and ministered in companies, it stands to reason that false prophets would, too. In fact, we find only three categories of prophets mentioned in the Old Testament: the false prophets of Baal and Asherah, and the true prophets of Jehovah.

Baal is a god of prophetic divination. This spirit leads people into idolatry through the guise of religion—just as it led the Israelites into idolatry when Moses was on the mountain talking with God. Remember when the children of Israel made a molten calf as an idol to worship? That was the spirit of Baal (see Exodus 32:8). Prophets of Baal, then, offer prophetic utterances that lead into idolatry. In other words, they lead people away from God to follow the selfish motives of their own hearts.

These were among Jezebel's puppets. Not much is said in the Bible about the specific function of these prophets, but we can assume that they were helping Jezebel move forward her religious agenda or she would not have kept them on her payroll.

What is idolatry? It is when you put something above God in your life. It is when you are devoted to something else more than to God. That could be a job, a relationship, money. Prophets of Baal, then, use divination to tap in to the idolatry in the human heart and prophesy what they find there through familiar spirits.

Listen now—if you go to a meeting and a prophet announces a special prayer line for all those who want to "sow" a thousand dollars in order to "harvest" financial breakthrough, a powerful prayer life, a restored relationship or anything of the like, then you are in the midst of Baal's camp. The Baal prophets network together and invite each other to their churches to merchandise their own sheep. They join together for large fundraisers that leave the sowers with empty pockets—pockets that will not be filled with anything other than the wrong motives they came to the altar with.

The spirit of Ashtoreth influences the prophets of Jezebel. Ashtoreth, also called Asherah, was the pagan god Queen Jezebel served. Ashtoreth was known as a seducing goddess of war. This is a different camp from the Baal prophets— and with a different motive. The prophets of Jezebel speak smooth, flattering words to manipulate and control. If that does not work, they transition into warfare mode and prophesy fearful things in order to control you. When you hear prophetic judgments and curses that are clearly not coming from the heart of God, you are dealing with one of Jezebel's modern-day prophets.

Just as Queen Jezebel spoke death threats in the Old Testament, so New Testament prophets who are consumed with the spirit of Jezebel continue to release death threats in the form of judgments and curses. Ashtoreth and Baal were married; these spirits often share one another's characteristics.

The third type of prophet is the prophet of Jehovah. In the New Testament, these are the Melchizedek prophets. New Testament prophets are not serving under the order of Aaron; they are serving under the order of Melchizedek just as Jesus did (see Hebrews 5:6–10). Jesus, our prototype Prophet, will not tolerate the spirit of Jezebel (control and manipulation through flattery and fear) or Baal worship (idolatry). If Jesus does not tolerate these spirits, we should not tolerate them either. We must look first at our own hearts, and purge ourselves of any common ground we have with these wicked spirits. Then we can begin to confront these dark powers and set captives free from the grip of deception.

Understanding Jezebel's Eunuchs

You know about Ahab, and you know about the 850 false prophets who ate at Jezebel's table, but are you familiar with Jezebel's eunuchs? The cast of Jezebel's puppet show includes eunuchs, so who are these spiritual servants? How do you recognize them? And how should you respond once you have identified Jezebel's eunuchs in your midst?

Discerning and dealing with Jezebel's eunuchs is part and parcel of defending against the work of this wicked spirit and its running mates of religion and witchcraft. We will explore this more fully in later chapters; I give you here an overview of the cast of characters.

The word *eunuch* comes from the Hebrew word *caric*, which means "to castrate." Jezebel wants to castrate you spiritually—strip you of your power. Jezebel does this by working with religion to muddy your identity in Christ and convince you that you cannot exercise your authority in Him because you made a mistake last week. So you begin speaking death instead of life over yourself—speaking the enemy's plan rather than God's plan—and essentially releasing word curses against your own life. Once you are spiritually weakened, Jezebel has you right where it wants you.

Throughout history eunuchs have been stigmatized in society. God commanded that any descendants of Aaron with a physical defect could not approach the altar to offer the "bread of . . . God" (Leviticus 21:8). That included a "man blind or lame, who has a marred face or any limb too long, a man who has a broken foot or broken hand, or is a hunchback or a dwarf, or a man who has a defect in his eye, or eczema or scab, or is a eunuch" (Leviticus 21:18–20). Everyone can now approach God's throne of grace boldly thanks to the blood of Jesus. But Jezebel is still deceiving saints to serve as eunuchs.

Historically speaking, eunuchs were often found in the households of kings, particularly in service in women's bedchambers. Eunuchs, for example, were custodians of the harem of virgins for King Xerxes (see Esther 2:3). Second Kings 9:32 mentions that eunuchs served in Jezebel's household. Eunuchs could be assigned to work in female bedchambers because they had been emasculated.

Serving in someone's bedroom gives access to intimate details of his or her life. Some modern-day eunuchs, in the spiritual rather than physical sense, thrive on this close relationship with the seductive Jezebel. Others are trapped through their own insecurities and fears—they need Jezebel. Either way, we need to learn to discern eunuchs in our midst. As with the topic of Ahab, if you research this topic of Jezebel and her eunuchs online, you will find some general information but not a lot of scriptural backing. Some say that eunuchs are Jezebel's spies, students or spiritual children, but there is no evidence of that in the Bible. Anecdotal descriptions like these can lead people into error, especially if they are undertaking a witch hunt for Jezebel's eunuchs.

I was once part of a congregation that was intensely focused on the spirit of Jezebel, and eventually her eunuchs. Essentially, anyone who was friendly with an individual whom the leaders had labeled "a Jezebel" was considered to be one of her "eunuchs" and shunned. This, as you can see, is a harmful approach. If someone really was flowing in a Jezebel spirit, and that one had "spiritual children" and "students" who served as spies, then godly spiritual leadership would seek to deliver them all from this spirit's clutches before trying to chase them out of the church.

All that said, Scripture indeed confirms that Queen Jezebel had eunuchs who attended her as servants, providing her comforts. Practically speaking, eunuchs today serve Jezebel's purposes knowingly, either because they are forced to or because they are seduced and deceived and choose to do so. In other words, eunuchs are aligned with Jezebel—sometimes by choice and sometimes by fearful duty—and execute her evil wishes.

Remember Maggie? The Jezebelic pastors told her she could go anywhere they went, so she learned intimate details of their lives, which gave her a greater sense of worth and elitism. Maggie was essentially serving in Jezebel's bedchamber. She worked overtime to make this Ahab pastor, who flowed equally in a Jezebel spirit, look good because she was seduced by the thimbleful of power he gave her.

But Maggie ultimately is not loyal to Pastor Jake, despite actually vowing loyalty for life during a special ceremony in front of the congregation. No, Maggie has sought help from other leaders. She experiences anxiety attacks before the Wednesday morning staff meetings because she knows she is going to be held accountable for things she cannot possibly control. She knows that she is being abused.

But at the same time she is conflicted: She continues to submit to the abuse because she wants the power that comes with serving in Jezebel's and Ahab's bedchambers.

It is likely that Queen Jezebel wielded her power over eunuchs with cruelty, because they were quick to throw her out the window to her death when help—in the form of Jehu— finally arrived (see 2 Kings 9:31–33). They served her, but ultimately they were not loyal to her. As Matthew Henry's Commentary puts it:

> Perhaps they had a secret dislike of Jezebel's wickedness, and hated her, though they served her; or, it may be, she was barbarous and injurious to those about her, and they were pleased with this opportunity of being avenged on her; or, observing Jehu's success, they hoped thus to ingratiate themselves with him, and keep their places in his court.

Eunuchs appear to be loyal to Jezebel, but many—and perhaps Maggie is among them—are just waiting for Jehu to come.

4

The Jehu Anointing

I have some understanding of Maggie's plight because I was in a battle with the spirits of Jezebel, religion and witchcraft for nearly eight years before I understood how this trio was slowly working to enslave me. By the time I discerned it, I was a top player in Jezebel's religious system in a local church that preached against these spirits at every turn.

Little did I know, in my zeal to serve God, that I had been deceived into building Jezebel's kingdom instead. See, like Maggie, I had hurts and wounds and a striving-for-religious-success mentality that my Jezebelic leaders discerned and pounced on. Less than two years old in Christ, I was given authority and ministry opportunities for which I was not spiritually or naturally prepared. And that made me ripe to play a starring role in Jezebel's puppet show in the local church.

My saving grace—and my way of escape—was my diligent pursuit of the truth. I loved God with all my heart, all my mind and all my strength. I studied the Word on my own. I worshiped and prayed in my prayer closet. I sought first the Kingdom of

God. As God healed my soul from the hurts of my past, it became progressively clear that something was amiss in my church. I began pointing out incidents of misuse of power, unjust accusations and downright spiritual abuse, but it was always explained away. Because I was so young in the Lord I accepted the excuses, until one day I could no longer deny the truth: Jezebel was running the church and I had to get out.

Ironically, it was this Jezebelic church that taught me how to break free. Because the church was so extremely focused on Jezebel, I actually used what that compromised church taught me to escape.

I mentioned a "Jehu anointing" in the last chapter. It is this mode of warfare that defeats the evil Jezebel spirit. You will remember that Jehu defeated Queen Jezebel when he told the eunuchs to throw her down from a window. He then trampled her body under his horse's hooves.

But I made a key mistake in my initial efforts to escape Jezebel's clutches.

What was my mistake? I rose up against it in an Elijah anointing instead of a Jehu anointing. Elijah defeated Jezebel's prophets on Mount Carmel when fire came down from heaven to consume the sacrifice, and Israel followed Elijah's directive to slay the false prophets. I followed after his example, battling against the false prophetic flow in the congregation—and I claimed victory. But I was not prepared for Jezebel and her witchcrafts to send me, like Elijah, running for the hills.

Let me mention here that we can choose what spirit to move in, based on the revelation we have. I did not have understanding of the Jehu anointing at this time, so I used the revelation I had. I was operating in the principles, you might say, of the way Elijah combated Jezebel, but I needed to be using Jehu's principles. They had different anointing, which is part of what led them to use the methods/strategies/principles they used.

The Elijah anointing took me only so far in the battle against Jezebel. I needed the Jehu anointing to defeat this wicked spirit in my life—and so do you. Indeed, I have had many small skirmishes with Jezebel, but I have also had a couple of showdowns with this wicked principality that have taught me the difference between moving in the spirit of Elijah and moving in the spirit of Jehu. There is a time, as with Elijah, to swing the sword of the Spirit in battle, but there is also a time, as with Jehu, to let the Lord do the warring for you (see 1 Samuel 17:47).

The Jehu anointing defeats Jezebel in your life, but you are likely to have more than one battle against this spirit. In other words, Jezebel will not be defeated once and for all until Jesus comes back—but you can defeat Jezebel every time it comes against you if you understand the secret to Jehu's success.

In this chapter, we will look at how Jehu confronted—and defeated—Jezebel. Specifically, he withstood her seductions, he did not give ear to witchcraft's intimidation, he did not fall for her deceptive words, and he did not try to defeat her alone (see 2 Kings 9:30–33). Jehu refused to negotiate with Jezebel. His only agenda was to obey the command of the Lord.

But we begin with the Elijah anointing for battle. Though he did not confront Jezebel herself, this great prophet battled her evil prophets and King Ahab face-to-face. One calling from the Lord on his life was teaching the Israelites that the Lord was God, and, by doing so, to confront and defeat the false prophets who were leading them into idolatry. When is this the right approach for us in the battle against Jezebel?

Elijah Swings the Sword of the Spirit

The Elijah anointing confronts misaligned church government and contends with false allegiances that woo people away from God. We like to talk about the spirit of Elijah in prophetic circles. Recall how, before the showdown at Mount Carmel, during which the prophet Elijah conquered the 850 false prophets in a spectacular demonstration of God's power, he asked the Israelites, "'How long will you falter between two opinions? If the LORD is God, follow Him; but if Baal, follow him.' But the people answered him not a word'" (1 Kings 18:21). Elijah went on to give the prophets of Baal a chance to prove that their idols were almighty. You know the story. The false prophets slaughtered a bull, put it on an altar and called on the name of their god from morning until noon. Baal did not answer. After Elijah mocked them, the false prophets started cutting themselves and prophesying until the evening. But Baal never responded (see 1 Kings 18:25–29).

When it was Elijah's turn, he repaired the altar of the Lord that was broken down, gathered twelve symbolic stones to build up the altar, dug a trench around it, put wood on it, cut a bull into pieces and put it on the altar, then drenched the offering and the wood with water—so much that water filled the trench. Elijah did not struggle or strain. He just lifted up a single prayer:

> "LORD God of Abraham, Isaac, and Israel, let it be known this day that You are God in Israel and I am Your servant, and that I have done all these things at Your word. Hear me, O LORD, hear me, that this people may know that You are the LORD God, and that You have turned their hearts back to You again."
>
> 1 Kings 18:36–37

The fire of the Lord fell and consumed the sacrifice, the wood, the stones and the dust—and licked up the water that was in the trench. The result: "Now when all the people saw it, they fell on their faces; and they said, 'The LORD, He is God! The LORD, He is God!'" (1 Kings 18:39). Then Elijah told the Israelites to seize the prophets of Baal, and he took them down to the brook and executed them.

The Elijah anointing turns the hearts of the fathers to the children, and the hearts of the children to their fathers (see Malachi 4:6). This heart-turning function is part and parcel of prophetic ministry. But this is not enough to conquer the influence of Jezebel. Let us not forget that Jezebel's intimidating death threats sent miracle-working Elijah running and wishing he could die (see 1 Kings 19:4). Ultimately, Elijah defeated the prophets of Baal, but Elijah did not defeat Jezebel.

Jezebel Will Not Repent

Jezebel's seductive influence in our lives must be torn down—and that requires the Jehu anointing. Whereas Elijah swung the sword of the Spirit in calling God's fire down from heaven, the Jehu anointing swings the sword of God's justice. Recall that King Ahab, the rock star idol, did more to provoke the Lord than all the kings of Israel before him. God used Jehu as an instrument of justice—but not before giving the evil king and queen a chance to repent.

After Elijah executed the prophets of Baal, Ahab ran back to Jezebel and told her everything that had happened—how the false prophets could not call down fire even after cutting themselves and prophesying for hours; how Elijah's simple prayer brought down fire from God that consumed the altar and everything around it; and how Elijah executed her prophets with the sword (see 1 Kings 19:1).

Notice that Ahab did not give glory to God; he gave glory to Elijah. Jezebel had massacred many prophets of the Lord, and Elijah brought a measure of justice by executing her false prophets. She did not see this as a judgment of God that might have caused her to tremble with fear and repent. She instead blamed Elijah. Ahab had likewise blamed Elijah—during the drought that had devastated the land. Before the showdown on Mount Carmel, he had called Elijah a "troubler of Israel" (1 Kings 18:17) rather than acknowledge the drought as God's judgment. Ahab was, thereby, elevating the prophet to godlike status. But it was really the God of Elijah they despised, even though they failed to recognize His efforts to get their attention. The power demonstration at Mount Carmel caused the people of Israel to repent and declare, "The LORD, He is God! The LORD, He is God!" (1 Kings 18:39). But not Ahab. This wicked king with his hard heart went running back to Jezebel to stir her up against Elijah so she could once again fight his battles for him.

Ahab is a provoker. He had provoked the Lord to righteous anger, and now he provoked Jezebel to murderous rage. She sent a messenger to Elijah to declare her oath: "So let the gods do to me, and more also, if I do not make your life as the life of one of them by tomorrow about this time" (1 Kings 19:2). Jezebel wanted revenge.

Jezebel's Response to Being Thwarted

Jezebel always wants revenge when you thwart its agenda. Jezebel's agenda is laid out clearly in Revelation 2:20: "To teach and seduce [Jesus'] servants to commit sexual immorality and eat things sacrificed to idols." In other words, Jezebel's goal is to lead believers into idolatry and sexual immorality. The spirit of Jezebel accomplished this goal in ancient Israel until Elijah came along and led many into repentance. Likewise, the spirit of Jezebel accomplished this goal in the church at Thyatira. And, much the same, Jezebel is accomplishing this goal in some churches today as pastors fall into sexual immorality and believers idolize careers, homes, families, sports, celebrities—and even their pastors.

And what happens when you thwart its agenda? Jezebel wants revenge. When you expose the operations of this spirit, Jezebel will work to intimidate you, discredit you and murder your reputation. I have experienced these tactics firsthand at the church I mentioned at the opening of this chapter. The church had a strong spiritual warfare bent. It preached, prayed and prophesied about Jezebel—literally. There was minimal teaching on the love of Christ, the grace of God—it was all about our authority in Christ, taking dominion and battling spirits.

In the Sermon on the Mount, Jesus promised that we could recognize people by their fruit:

> "Beware of false prophets, who come to you in sheep's clothing, but inwardly they are ravenous wolves. You will know them by their fruits. Do men gather grapes from thornbushes or figs from thistles? Even so, every good tree bears good fruit, but a bad tree bears bad fruit. . . . Therefore by their fruits you will know them."
>
> Matthew 7:15–17, 20

You can also judge church leadership by the fruit of its faithful followers. Well, the faithful followers of this church—as well as its staff and governing body—were bearing rotten fruit.

Girls on the worship team were getting pregnant. Altar workers were stealing money from people in the church to support their crack cocaine habits. Several in leadership were arrested for fabricating license plates and driving with expired driver's licenses. Illegal immigrants were brought on staff and secretly paid low wages. The Federal Trade Commission investigated some members for financial fraud. Others were coming to church drunk. The list goes on and on—and on and on.

In the environment of Jezebel, power and deception rule. When my eyes were finally opened, and I pointed out the glaring problems, I became the problem. Leadership turned against me. I was stripped of my opportunities to teach, stripped of my oversight of ministries within the church—and attempts were made to strip my very identity in Christ by trying to paint me with the brush of rebellion in order to identify me as belonging to Jezebel.

That is how Jezebel works. If you do not cooperate with this spirit, it gets revenge by trying to disgrace you. Jezebel's goal is to deflect the attention from itself and turn you into the enemy who is rocking the sinful boat.

Jezebel Will Be Judged

Jesus promised that judgment is the result wherever repentance is absent. He told the church at Thyatira how much He appreciated their works, love, service, faith and patience. But He had one thing against them: They tolerated Jezebel. They tolerated a spirit of seduction that wooed blood-bought believers in the congregation into immorality and idolatry. Let's listen to the words of our Savior:

> "Nevertheless I have a few things against you, because you allow that woman Jezebel, who calls herself a prophetess, to teach and seduce My servants to commit sexual immorality and eat things sacrificed to idols. And I gave her time to repent of her sexual immorality, and she did not repent. Indeed I will cast her into a sickbed, and those who commit adultery with her into great tribulation, unless they repent of their deeds. I will kill her children with death, and all the churches shall know that I am He who searches the minds and hearts. And I will give to each one of you according to your works."
>
> Revelation 2:20–23

Jesus' judgment against Jezebel is similar to that of the religious spirit–driven scribes and Pharisees whom He called hypocrites and serpents. Let's do a quick comparison. Jesus said they would receive greater condemnation and asked, "How can you escape the condemnation of hell?" (Matthew 23:14, 33). The answer is clear: They could repent. And some of the Pharisees did repent. Among the most famed Pharisees who repented—a true persecutor of the Church—was the apostle Paul (see Acts 9). He later called himself the chief of sinners, and serves as our example of how God can work with all who repent, no matter what horrible acts they have undertaken.

Repentance was available for the Thyatira Jezebel. Jesus states that He "gave her time to repent of her sexual immorality, and she did not repent" (Revelation 2:21). God also gave Queen Jezebel from the Old Testament a space to repent. The showdown at Mount Carmel should have triggered a change of heart. But Queen Jezebel would not repent. The spirit of Jezebel will not repent. If this spirit is attacking you or flowing through you, you have to rise up in a Jehu anointing—not an Elijah anointing—to conquer it.

Jehu Wields the Sword of Justice

God commissioned Elijah to anoint Jehu as king of Israel (see 1 Kings 19:16–17). Just as Saul was still on the throne when Samuel anointed David, so Ahab was on the throne when God announced that a new king was to be anointed. It was actually Elisha, the successor of Elijah, who directed the anointing of Jehu, sending a man from the company of the prophets with specific instructions (see 2 Kings 9:1–3).

Who was Jehu? What God-given traits did he carry, and what anointing did he receive that led him to victory over Ahab's household—and Jezebel?

Jehu was a commander of the king's forces at Ramoth Gilead at the time that Elisha directed his anointing. In other words, Jehu was already a warrior at heart. In order to conquer Jezebel (and Ahab) we need to be willing to war in the spirit. Unlike Jehu we are not wrestling against flesh and blood. We are not battling a physical Ahab and a physical Jezebel. Even if that spirit is operating through people, our battle is not with those human personalities; our battle is with the principality.

But we also know that the battle is the Lord's. Paul wrote:

> For we do not wrestle against flesh and blood, but against principalities, against powers, against the rulers of the darkness of this age, against spiritual hosts of wickedness in the heavenly places. Therefore take up the whole armor of God, that you may be able to withstand in the evil day, and having done all, to stand.
>
> Ephesians 6:12–13

When we battle Jezebel, we battle a principality—and we need to be sure to do so in the strength and wisdom of the Lord and for His glory.

One of Elisha's spiritual children was charged with anointing Jehu as king, and this commissioning is telling. Let's listen in:

> And [one from the company of the prophets] poured the oil on [Jehu's] head, and said to him, "Thus says the LORD God of Israel: 'I have anointed you king over the people of the LORD, over Israel. You shall strike down the house of Ahab your master, that I may avenge the blood of My servants the prophets, and the blood of all the servants of the LORD, at the hand of Jezebel. For the whole house of Ahab shall perish; and I will cut off from Ahab all the males in Israel, both bond and free. So I will make the house of Ahab like

the house of Jeroboam the son of Nebat, and like the house
of Baasha the son of Ahijah. The dogs shall eat Jezebel on
the plot of ground at Jezreel, and there shall be none to bury
her.'" And he opened the door and fled.

2 Kings 9:6–10

When Ahab and Jezebel did not respond to the drought and
the execution of the false prophets during Elijah's prophetic
tenure, God raised up a warrior to bring greater judgment
against them. Jehu was given the task of destroying the whole
house of Ahab, which included Jezebel's children.

Notice that Jesus' prophetic words over Jezebel, the woman
who called herself a prophetess in the church of Thyatira, are
congruent with Jehu's charge. Jesus told the Thyatira church,
"Indeed I will cast her into a sickbed, and those who commit
adultery with her into great tribulation, unless they repent
of their deeds. I will kill her children with death" (Revelation
2:22–23). Jezebel cursed herself when she declared to Elijah,
"So let the gods do to me, and more also, if I do not make
your life as the life of one of them by tomorrow about this
time" (1 Kings 19:2).

Well, we know that Jezebel's oath against Elijah failed.
She did not succeed in taking Elijah's life, and she opened
the door to her own doom. Elijah did not finish off Jezebel,
but he had a hand in her demise, as he was charged with
anointing the man who would bring her down.

Notice that the judgment spoken through Elijah did not
happen right away. God's judgments do not always come
when we think they should. That is why it is so dangerous to
think that all is well in your life or in a ministry just because
prosperity continues. God is longsuffering. Jesus gave the
Thyatira Jezebel space to repent, and He gives people flowing
in the Jezebel spirit space to repent also.

After Jezebel cursed herself, nothing seemed to have changed. All seemed to be going well in the kingdom: Ahab was victorious in battle (see 1 Kings 20:21) and Jezebel continued in her witchcrafts (see 1 Kings 21:7). It was not until Ahab was killed in battle, Elijah was taken up into heaven and Elisha gave the command to anoint Jehu as king of Israel that judgment fell on Ahab's house (see 2 Kings 9–10).

Jehu Stands Against Jezebel's Weapons

The unrepentant Jezebel received advance warning that the newly anointed Jehu was arriving in Jezreel—and she knew he was coming with a vengeance.

God's judgment had started with Jezebel's son King Joram, which ironically means "Jehovah is exalted." We noted earlier the question Joram had asked Jehu: "'Is it peace, Jehu?' And he answered, 'What peace, so long as the harlotries of your mother Jezebel and her witchcrafts are so many?'" (2 Kings 9:22 NASB). Joram had tried to flee at that point, but Jehu's arrow had hit him between the shoulders and had sunk into his heart. Jehu had then commanded his captain to throw Joram's body into Naboth's field. Justice was served for Naboth.

Just as Jezebel heard about the slaying of the false prophets at Mount Carmel, she also heard of her son's death (see 2 Kings 9:30). In her fearless pride and mockery of God's justice, Jezebel did not back down from a fight—but she does not fight with natural weapons, either. Instead of humbling herself and repenting, Jezebel used her first weapon: She decided to try to seduce the newly anointed king. After all, she had seduced Ahab into her idolatry, why not Jehu?

The Bible says that when Jezebel heard that Jehu was coming she "put paint on her eyes and adorned her head, and looked through a window" (2 Kings 9:30). Just as the Thyatira Jezebel worked to seduce God's servants into immorality and idolatry, Queen Jezebel was working to seduce Jehu into her clan. With Ahab and her son dead, she saw seducing the new king as her best opportunity to stay in power. But Jehu was not deceived. Seduction is always Jezebel's first move. When that fails she will next try witchcraft's intimidation. Jezebel's threats had worked to frighten Elijah, so she decided to use the same tactic with Jehu. Often, Jezebel's intimidation comes with accusation. The point is to deflect the attention from its wrongdoing and allege wrongdoing against you. The goal is to get you to rise up to defend yourself instead of allowing God to vindicate you. When you take matters into your own hands, you begin to war in your own strength. We cannot defeat Jezebel without God's help.

Jezebel spoke this accusation against Jehu: "Is it peace, Zimri, murderer of your master?" (2 Kings 9:31). By addressing Jehu as *Zimri*, Jezebel was making a comparison. Some years earlier, Zimri had been commander of half the chariots of Elah, then king of Israel. Having conspired against his sovereign, Zimri had killed the drunken Elah and taken his place on the throne (see 1 Kings 16:8–10). Thus, Jezebel was labeling Jehu as a traitor, a rebel, one overtaking the throne by treachery and force rather than by a calling from God.

This was an especially nasty accusation against Jehu—and untrue. But Jehu did not dignify Jezebel's witchcraft intimidation with an answer. He did not fall for her deceptive words.

Notice, too, how Jezebel worked here with religion. The religious spirit twists the Word of God to make it mean something it does not. The Pharisees did this by interpreting the Word through a legalistic view rather than understanding the spirit of the Law. When Jesus said things like, "It has been said . . . but I say to you . . . ," He was not rewriting Scripture; He was explaining the spirit of the Law. The legalistic religious spirit tries to hold you to a literal interpretation without a revelation of the spirit behind it. Religion, then, tried to get Jehu to second-guess himself and his discernment by suggesting he had not heard God correctly. "Did God really say that?" is what the serpent said to Eve.

Jehu did not second-guess what God had directed him to do just because Jezebel was chattering against him. That is the strategy we have to take when Jezebel's accusations are flying against us. Let God deal with it. Like Jehu, we have to know that we know that we know that God has spoken, and act on what He says.

Jehu never said a word to Jezebel. He did not holler at Jezebel at the top of his lungs or warn her of her fate. Clearly, he saw her up there in the window and heard what she was saying, but her words did not move him.

Jehu ignored her tactics; then he took action. Notice an important aspect of his response: Jehu did not try to defeat Jezebel alone. He recruited some of those who were closest to the wicked queen to help him. "And he looked up at the window, and said, 'Who is on my side? Who?' So two or three eunuchs looked out at him" (2 Kings 9:32). This is an important principle in defeating the Jezebel spirit—get reinforcements.

Jehu was essentially asking, "Whose side are you on— Jehovah's or Jezebel's?" Once Jehu saw that he had reinforcements, he told the eunuchs to throw her down. From this we see that at least three of Jezebel's eunuchs were not loyal to her wicked majesty.

> So they threw her down, and some of her blood spattered on the wall and on the horses; and he trampled her underfoot. [He later said,] "Go now, see to this accursed woman, and bury her, for she was a king's daughter." So they went to bury her, but they found no more of her than the skull and the feet and the palms of her hands. Therefore they came back

and told him. And he said, "This is the word of the LORD, which He spoke by His servant Elijah the Tishbite, saying, 'On the plot of ground at Jezreel dogs shall eat the flesh of Jezebel; and the corpse of Jezebel shall be as refuse on the surface of the field, in the plot at Jezreel, so that they shall not say, "Here lies Jezebel."'"

2 Kings 9:33–37

Maybe you realize that you have given in to Jezebel in your own life. Repenting is the right way out. And confessing your sins to others so that you may be healed is your safety net (see James 5:16). Jezebel will certainly come back and try to seduce you again. Having strong believers stand with you to help you battle the next round is wisdom. If Jezebel is coming against you, and you find yourself in a fierce battle, get reinforcements as Jehu did. There is no shame in asking for help; humble warriors look for backup.

Jehu never negotiated with her. He never gave in to her intimidation. He never defended himself against her accusations. He did not want or need anything from Jezebel. His only agenda was to obey the command of the Lord.

When our only agenda is to obey the command of the Lord, we can defeat Jezebel at every turn. Obedience guards us from Jezebel's false religious system because we refuse to bow down to idols. Likewise, obedience guards us from Jezebel's witchcrafts because we will be "casting down imaginations and every high thing that exalteth itself against the knowledge of God" (2 Corinthians 10:5 KJV).

Avoiding Jehu's Mistakes

Jehu went on to wipe out the entire house of Ahab. He commanded the slaughter of Ahab's seventy sons and all who remained in Ahab's house in Jezreel—all his great men, his close acquaintances and his priests (see 2 Kings 10:1–11). Next, he killed 42 brothers of Ahaziah, king of Judah, because they were coming to greet the families of Ahab and Jezebel (see 2 Kings 10:12–14). From there, he killed all who remained loyal to Ahab in Samaria (see 2 Kings 10:15–17). Then he targeted the Baal worshipers (see 2 Kings 10:18–28).

Jehu fulfilled Elijah's prophecy. You would think that he would have continued on as one of the most righteous kings of Israel after such stunning victories, but he did not. Jehu fell into some of the same sins Ahab had promoted! The Bible says, "Jehu did not turn away from the sins of Jeroboam the son of Nebat, who had made Israel sin, that is, from the golden calves that were at Bethel and Dan" (2 Kings 10:29). And, "Jehu took no heed to walk in the law of the Lord God of Israel with all his heart; for he did not depart from the sins of Jeroboam, who had made Israel sin" (2 Kings 10:31).

What is the lesson here? Anyone, even the greatest spiritual warrior, can fall into idolatry. We have to guard our hearts, especially after great victories, and remember that we are instruments in God's hands. The battle—even against Jezebel, her religious idolatry and her witchcrafts—is the Lord's.

5

Witchcraft's Wicked Power

There are two times every year when I wind up completely exhausted—without any natural reason for it. I sleep plenty. I drink lots of water. I exercise. Yet even after getting a full night of rest I wake up tempted to shut the alarm off, pull the covers over my head and continue sleeping. And there was a time when I did just that. There was a time when I could not make it through the day without feeling so oppressed that I took midday naps only to wake up feeling worse.

Before I got the revelation that I am sharing with you I truly wondered what was wrong with me. Even now, every October and every spring I battle those same feelings. I am grateful that the Holy Spirit offers a friendly reminder about the spiritual climate and what is going on in the heavenlies: It is witchcraft. Wicked witchcraft. Rick Joyner has one of the best definitions of *witchcraft*, explaining how it uses a spirit other than the Holy Spirit to dominate, manipulate and control others.

Jezebel operates in false spiritual authority—the wicked queen usurped Ahab's authority, for instance, when she gave the order to murder God's prophets. Jezebel also persuaded Ahab to lead Israel into idolatry and immorality. This rebellion against God's Law, as we have seen, is the same as the sin of witchcraft (see 1 Samuel 15:23). Witchcraft takes on many different forms and degrees, whether voodoo or Wicca or word curses.

I live in South Florida, and witchcraft is a stronghold that marks the spiritual climate here year-round. Miami is home to a cornucopia of cultural rebellion through homosexuality, an active drug scene, naughty nightclubs and the like, as well as a diverse population that has brought Santeria from Cuba, voodoo from Haiti and Rastafarianism from Jamaica to our shores. You might say the principalities and powers here are as eclectic as the population. But there are two times of the year when it intensifies: during Lent when witchcraft deifies Mary, the mother of Jesus, and during the Halloween season when Wiccans kick their witchcraft into overdrive. I believe the same holds true in many cities across the world.

It seems fairly obvious for witchcraft to intensify during the occult celebration of Halloween, but the observance of Lent—at least in South Florida—is no different. The spirit of witchcraft gets so thick those weeks before Easter it seems you have to cut through it with a power saw.

We know it is not God's will for Mary to be worshiped—or prayed to—as a member of the Godhead. My experience living here over the past decade demonstrates how Mary-worship empowers the Jezebel spirit and its witchcrafts.

In some religions Mary is referred to as the "queen of heaven." What does the Bible say about the "queen of heaven"? Ashtoreth, the chief pagan goddess of war and sex mentioned in the Old Testament, was known as the queen of heaven.

The Bible notes that the people of Judah were provoking God to anger by offering sacrifices to this goddess, hoping to win her favor (see Jeremiah 7:18; 44:17). Ashtoreth was the goddess of the Sidonians (see 1 Kings 11:5). Jezebel's father was king of the Sidonians (see 1 Kings 16:31). It is the Ashtoreth spirit that is behind Jezebel's witchcrafts.

Can you connect the dots?

Spiritual witchcraft is a spiritual force that might cause you to feel like giving up. It can make you feel physically exhausted and even spark symptoms of infirmities. The imaginations hitting your mind become more intense. Indeed, witchcraft can cause you to grow weary in well-doing and even faint if you do not know what you are dealing with—and how to battle it. I will share more with you about how to battle witchcraft in the next chapter, but first we need to understand the origin of spiritual witchcraft, how word curses work in the spirit realm, how witchcraft releases imaginations and how the spirits of Jezebel and religion use witchcraft to hold believers in bondage.

The Origin of Spiritual Witchcraft

Consider what the Bible says about witchcraft. It might surprise you to learn that what most people—even Wiccans—call witchcraft is not always the same as what the Bible calls witchcraft. When you think of witchcraft, for example, you probably think of black magic or conjuring the dead. Those abominations are discussed in the Bible. But witchcraft is not always so mysterious. Indeed, rebellion, word curses and works of the flesh also fall into the realm of witchcraft. However you define it, though, practicing witchcraft is a serious sin, and far more Christians are experts at this than you might realize.

Spiritual witchcraft is common, even in the church, because it taps in to the death-and-life-producing power of the tongue. Remember, witchcraft works to dominate, manipulate or control others. Practically speaking, when someone uses flattery, intimidation, manipulation or some other emotional tactic to pressure you or cause you guilt, it is a form of witchcraft.

The preacher who hypes up the offering with promises of breakthrough when you sow your financial seed quickly—as if God's promise will expire if you do not have the money on you right now—is operating in a low level of witchcraft. When salesmen smooth talk customers in order to seal a deal, it is essentially witchcraft. When men seduce women sexually—or women seduce men sexually—they are tapping in to Jezebel's witchcraft. The common denominator in all of these examples is people using words to get what they want rather than praying and asking God to supply what they need.

We are all susceptible to tapping in to witchcraft—and even releasing it over our own lives—through our words. The Bible says, "We all often stumble and fall and offend in many things. And if anyone does not offend in speech [never says the wrong things], he is a fully developed character and a perfect man, able to control his whole body and to curb his entire nature" (James 3:2 AMPLIFIED). James goes on to give the example of putting a small bit in a horse's mouth: It allows any one of us to control the direction of that thousand-pound beast.

Here is how that works: When the rider pulls a rein, the bit presses on the tongue and applies pressure to the horse's gums, which contain sensitive nerve endings. That causes the horse to turn in the direction the rider wants him to go to alleviate the pressure. If you have ever been under demonic pressure, you understand how it presses on your tongue. When we are under pressure of any kind, our carnal nature is more likely to manifest. We are more likely to say something that does not agree with God's Word. We are more likely to say out loud the thoughts the enemy is using to put pressure on our tongues. When we speak the enemy's plans out of our mouths, we are releasing witchcraft.

Witchcraft's Power of Death

We can change the course of our lives, for better or worse, with the power that is in the tongue. Notice again that Proverbs 18:21 says, "Death and life are in the power of the tongue, and those who love it will eat its fruit." We often misquote that Scripture, saying that "the power of death and life are in the tongue." You may not think it matters, but it does. It is the tongue that has the power, and the undisciplined, or fleshly, person is more likely to wield death with that power than life. If you do not believe that, then just start listening to how people in your workplace—or in your church—talk. Are those frustrating words releasing life or death? How about the gossip, defensive speech, angry words?

There is a good reason why Jesus said, "For every idle word men may speak, they will give account of it in the day of judgment. For by your words you will be justified, and by your words you will be condemned" (Matthew 12:37). We can release words that make ourselves or those around us feel condemned. Since there is "no condemnation to those who are in Christ Jesus, who do not walk according to the flesh, but according to the Spirit" (Romans 8:1), we know those words are not coming from the Spirit of God. Those words are coming from our flesh, which can release witchcraft (see Galatians 5:19–20).

Spiritual witchcraft relies on the power that is in our tongues—and other people's tongues—to release its attacks. Like a bit in a horse's mouth, James also explained,

> Even so the tongue is a little member and boasts great things. See how great a forest a little fire kindles! And the tongue is a fire, a world of iniquity. The tongue is so set among our members that it defiles the whole body, and sets on fire the course of nature; and it is set on fire by hell.
>
> For every kind of beast and bird, of reptile and creature of the sea, is tamed and has been tamed by mankind. But no man can tame the tongue. It is an unruly evil, full of deadly poison. With it we bless our God and Father, and with it we curse men, who have been made in the similitude of God. Out of the same mouth proceed blessing and cursing. My brethren, these things ought not to be so. Does a spring send forth fresh water and bitter from the same opening? Can a fig tree, my brethren, bear olives, or a grapevine bear figs? Thus no spring yields both salt water and fresh.
>
> James 3:5–12

The good news is the Holy Spirit can help us tame our tongues. Over time, we will mature in this area as we work to release life instead of death—and the witchcraft curses that accompany words of death.

The challenge, then, becomes other people. People, whether believers or unbelievers, who are operating in a religious spirit or a Jezebel spirit are expert at releasing witchcraft's power of death over their targets. Typically, they have no idea what they are doing.

Rebellion Is Like the Sin of Witchcraft

I believe our own rebellion—beyond words—can also open the door to witchcraft attacks in our lives. Often it is our own self-ambition, which is a form of idolatry, that can cause us to disobey the Word.

Remember how King Saul was ordered to utterly destroy the Amalekites and everything they had: man, woman, infant and suckling, ox and sheep, camel and ass? Saul found victory in battle against Israel's enemy by the grace of God, but failed to obey the voice of God when the dust settled. He spared Agag, the king of the Amalekites, and kept the best of the livestock (see 1 Samuel 15:1–9). God quickly took notice of his greed, which the Bible calls idolatry (see Colossians 3:5).

> Now the word of the LORD came to Samuel, saying, "I greatly regret that I have set up Saul as king, for he has turned back from following Me, and has not performed My commandments." And it grieved Samuel, and he cried out to the LORD all night. So when Samuel rose early in the morning to meet Saul, it was told Samuel, saying, "Saul went to Carmel, and indeed, he set up a monument for himself; and he has gone on around, passed by, and gone down to Gilgal."
>
> 1 Samuel 15:10–12

I had read this account many, many times before the words *he set up a monument for himself* leaped off the page at me. Can you imagine disobeying God and then setting up a monument to yourself, essentially to celebrate your disobedience?

Many of us have done this. Maybe God told you not to buy a home for another year, but you found a great price on your dream house so you bought it anyway. You disobeyed God and set up a monument to your disobedience—one you could be paying off for decades. Our self-ambition and greed, which are idolatry, can often lead us into rebellion, which is as bad as witchcraft, and can release witchcraft over our lives.

As with Saul, witchcraft clouds our minds so that we cannot see what we are doing wrong. When Samuel arrived, the king had the nerve to tell the prophet, "Blessed are you of the LORD! I have performed the commandment of the LORD" (1 Samuel 15:13). What happened? Saul was a hearer of the Word but not a doer of the Word. He deceived himself (see James 1:22). But God was not mocked and Samuel was not fooled by the excuses Saul made:

> "I have obeyed the voice of the LORD, and gone on the mission on which the LORD sent me, and brought back Agag king of Amalek; I have utterly destroyed the Amalekites. But the people took of the plunder, sheep and oxen, the best of the things which should have been utterly destroyed, to sacrifice to the LORD your God in Gilgal."
>
> 1 Samuel 15:20–21

Saul was so stubborn that at first he refused to admit his disobedience. He actually justified his actions, saying that he was planning to use the forbidden items in sacrifices. Only after Samuel rebuked Saul a second time, with harsher words, did he catch the revelation. And in the prophet's rebuke we see a definition of witchcraft:

> And Samuel said, Hath the LORD as great delight in burnt offerings and sacrifices, as in obeying the voice of the LORD? Behold, to obey is better than sacrifice, and to hearken than the fat of rams. For rebellion is as the sin of witchcraft, and stubbornness is as iniquity and idolatry. Because thou hast rejected the word of the LORD, he hath also rejected thee from being king.
>
> And Saul said unto Samuel, I have sinned: for I have transgressed the commandment of the LORD, and thy words: because I feared the people, and obeyed their voice.
>
> 1 Samuel 15:22–24 KJV

In that rebuke—and in Saul's penitence—we find one way that Christians are practicing sin in the realm of witchcraft:

through rebellion that arises when self-ambition and fear of man are greater than the fear of the Lord. This is one of the reasons why King Solomon warned that "the fear of man brings a snare" (Proverbs 29:25). When we start moving in our own covetousness or reacting based on the fear of man rather than the fear of the Lord, we are more likely to tap in to witchcraft through control and manipulation. Even little hints of manipulation, flattery or pushiness toward one's own agenda can open the door to witchcraft.

Rebellion in and of itself is not witchcraft, but witchcraft is a form of rebellion against God. The Word forbids the practice of witchcraft, so to tap in to witchcraft is to rebel against God. When we flow in rebellion, we are opening ourselves to the realm of the demonic. Rebellion of drunkenness, for instance, opens the door to spirits of addiction. Rebellion of watching pornography opens the door to the spirit of immorality.

How Word Curses Work

Then there is Jezebel's witchcraft. Look once again at 2 Kings 9:22. Just before the wicked queen's demise, Jehu offered insight into an open door for the Jezebel spirit when he told her son, "What peace, so long as the whoredoms of thy mother Jezebel and her witchcrafts [Hebrew: *sorcery*] are so many?" (KJV). Again, the spirit of Jezebel is essentially a spirit of seduction that works to escort believers into immorality and idolatry. And this spirit uses witchcraft against its enemies.

Jezebel's witchcraft was rooted in rebellion, but the type of witchcraft in this verse refers to incantations and spells. In the modern church world, we call them word curses. When Jezebel sent the word curse to Elijah, promising his death, she released a spirit of fear. This spirit released witchcraft imaginations against Elijah's mind. Elijah then *saw* the outcome. Elijah imagined her words coming to pass—he imagined the curse as true.

Maybe you can relate to witchcraft imaginations that are released against your mind through word curses. God gave us a holy imagination to use for His glory, but Scripture reveals repeatedly that man uses his imagination for evil (see Genesis 6:5; Proverbs 6:18; Jeremiah 3:17; Luke 1:51). The propensity for an unrenewed mind to meditate on that which is not good is to witchcraft's advantage.

As holy as Elijah was, and despite his powerful anointing, Jezebel's witchcraft sent him running for his life. By leaving his servant behind, he effectively isolated himself from those who could speak truth to him—another tactic of Jezebel. The mighty Elijah actually sat down under a broom tree and prayed that he would die. "It is enough! Now, LORD, take my life, for I am no better than my fathers!" (1 Kings 19:4). Then he went to sleep. As I mentioned earlier, exhaustion and feeling like giving up are signs of a witchcraft attack, which we will explore more deeply later in this chapter. Elijah took a long nap, woke up to eat and went right back to bed! All this after Jezebel released a word curse and spirit of fear against him that set his imagination—and his feet—running into the wilderness.

In modern times, word curses are not always so dramatic—people rarely, if ever, threaten our lives. But word curses are just as real, if not as severe. When we speak negatively—"She will never hold down a job acting like that"; "That marriage is bound to fail the way he treats her"; "The doctors said he's going to die within thirty days. Isn't that sad?"; "I catch that flu every year!"; "I'll never get a raise at this dead-end job"—we are agreeing with the enemy's plan and giving power to it with our anointed mouths. When we speak word curses over someone's life—or our own—we are opening the door to the devil. Death and life are in the power of the tongue. If you are inadvertently—or purposely—releasing witchcraft over people with the words of your mouth, repent and get your mouth back in line with the Spirit of God.

Discerning a Witchcraft Attack

The spirits of Jezebel and religion use witchcraft to keep us in bondage. In order to combat this spiritual trio and its effects, we need first to discern what spirits are actually operating.

Although there is no lack of checklists that we can tick down like a doctor diagnosing a disease, it can be difficult to deduce naturally what spirit is truly operating in the spiritual climate—whether it is a religious spirit or a Jezebel spirit or witchcraft. That is because these spirits share similar characteristics. Jezebel, after all, is religious and needs the system of religion to flow through. Religion is controlling, yet Jezebel often uses control to get the job done. A person flowing in a religious spirit or a Jezebel spirit can release witchcraft with words.

There is a vast difference between discernment and deduction. Using deduction in spiritual warfare is dangerous. We need the gift of discernment to understand what we are battling. We cannot take authority over false authority in the name of Jesus if we cannot discern what we are taking authority over. Sure, there are the generic "I bind every spirit that is not of Christ, in the name of Jesus!" prayers, but my experience tells me those will take you only so far in battle.

Flowing in suspicion or making general deductions can lead to false accusations that leave people in bondage on both sides of the battlefield. In other words, you think you are dealing with a religious spirit, but the person is not delivered because she is flowing in a Jezebel spirit. Or your mind is under attack with witchcraft's imaginations, and you do not overcome because you are focused on a spirit of fear when Jezebel is the true culprit.

Paul talks about fighting—but not as one who beats the air (see 1 Corinthians 9:26). When you are beating the air, you clearly are not hitting your target—and you are wearing yourself out in combat against the wrong enemy while the unseen enemy continues attacking. Written in the sixth century BC, Sun Tzu's classic *The Art of War* offers an interesting idea that we can apply to spiritual warfare today:

> Hence the saying: If you know the enemy and know yourself, you need not fear the result of a hundred battles. If you know yourself but not the enemy, for every victory gained you will also suffer a defeat. If you know neither the enemy nor yourself, you will succumb in every battle.

Satan can take advantage of us when we are ignorant of his devices (see 2 Corinthians 2:11). That does not mean we should keep our focus on the devil, but we should not ignore the devil either. In spiritual warfare we need to know what enemy we are fighting—we need to discern what spirit is coming against us through the wisdom of the Holy Ghost. We also need to know ourselves. We need to know who we are in Christ and understand our authority in Christ. In a later chapter, we will learn more about how the spirit of religion works to prevent you from receiving a revelation of who you are in Christ and your authority in Him so that Jezebel and witchcraft (and other spiritual enemies, for that matter) can keep you in bondage.

With all that said, I did mention a few of the symptoms of spiritual witchcraft I have experienced personally—and symptoms others I know have reported to me—that were broken off when we came against the attack with mighty God-given weapons. I will talk more about those weapons in the next chapter. For now, let's review how to discern a witchcraft attack. What are the symptoms that you are getting hit with witchcraft? Exhaustion is one of them. Fear is another. Then there are racing imaginations of bad things, feeling like giving up, depression and isolating yourself from those who can help you break the curse.

Elijah experienced all of these symptoms. Of course, these symptoms can come from other attacks—or just as part of our emotional makeup in response to life events or genuine physical maladies. But when they come all at once like a flood, it is a good indication that witchcraft is working against us. Ask the Holy Spirit for confirmation of what you are sensing in the natural. If you discern it is witchcraft, pick up your mighty weapons and start warring. I will show you how in the next chapter.

6

Casting Down
Witchcraft's Curses

We might expect curses to come through the spoken word—malicious gossip from the lips of another Christian is one example. But an actual physical assault from someone flowing in a Jezebel spirit gives literal meaning to wrestling principalities and powers, rulers of the darkness of this age and spiritual hosts of wickedness in the heavenly places (see Ephesians 6:12)!

Indeed, when a demon attacks and curses you physically through someone who has yielded to evil influence, a wrestling match with the flesh and blood that is hosting the foul spirit can ensue.

I have had several of these experiences with people seeking deliverance, and I have witnessed many more. Some of these precious ones manifested the witchcraft with strength that far surpassed their human stature. On one occasion, a spirit of fear expressed itself so strongly through a 110-pound woman that it took five people—including two men—to restrain her while commanding the spirit to bow in the name of Jesus (see Philippians 2:10).

This type of activity is shown in Scripture. The man in the country of the Gadarenes was controlled by an unclean spirit that "often seized him, and he was kept under guard, bound with chains and shackles; and he broke the bonds and was driven by the demon into the wilderness" (Luke 8:29). Those demons gave him supernatural strength to break through chains and bonds! After Jesus cast the demon out, the man sat at His feet, clothed and in his right mind.

Despite many years of participating in deliverance ministry, though, I had never experienced anything quite like what I am about to share. It is a good example of how Jezebel uses Christians—or those who at least claim to be saved by the grace of God through faith in Jesus—to release witchcraft curses. Although you will probably never face this type of demonic attack, the principles you will learn about casting down the curses of Jezebel, religion and witchcraft will work at any level of spiritual warfare.

When Jezebel Manifests

The story began on the day of a special prophetic event. The atmosphere was charged with God's presence. The service was bathed in prayer and worship for 48 continuous hours leading up to the Sunday morning gathering. The leadership—from several different ministries—was in perfect harmony. Every gift was in its place and the anointing was flowing. We all expected a great move of God. When God begins moving, however, demons often begin manifesting in order to try to counter it. We expected that, but not in the way it panned out.

We were worshiping the Lord—I was scheduled to preach in a few minutes—when I heard someone begin praying loudly in what sounded like a demonic language. I looked and saw that a wild-eyed woman had come to the altar and was standing behind a visiting leader from another nation. I discerned the spirit of Jezebel releasing witchcraft.

The visiting minister kept her stance silently. I looked around hoping to dispatch an usher to lead the woman out, but it was evident that no one in the young church had been in this type of situation before. They looked stunned.

I walked over and gently nudged the wild-eyed woman, and asked her to sit down. This woman was often disruptive within the congregation. She had not been assigned to the altar and had no authority to lay hands on anyone.

Instead of leaving, she gripped the minister by her shoulders. When she refused to loosen her strong grip, I took her arm and began to pull her away. She held tight and refused to let go. I would not relent, and said so, in the name of Jesus.

That is when she suddenly let go of the minister and lunged toward me. She smacked me in the head with her hand and began spewing forth witchcraft curses. It was a literal wrestling match at the altar! Although it was intense, it only lasted seconds because the demon had to bow at the name of Jesus.

The woman stopped, turned and walked out of the sanctuary. It caused quite a stir.

Extreme Witchcraft Attacks

Again, this kind of battle is well documented in Scripture. Jesus cast out devils everywhere He went, and some of those devils caused violent reactions in the people hosting them before they came out at His command. When Jesus cast an unclean spirit out of a man in the synagogue, for example, the spirit first convulsed his human host and then cried out with a shriek (see Mark 1:25–26). On another occasion, a demon was throwing a boy down and convulsing him (see Luke 9:42). Still another time, a demon threw the man down before finally coming out (see Luke 4:33–35). And we have already noted the demonized man from the Gadarenes.

Whenever you encounter these types of demonic attacks, you have to think quickly. It is true that "no weapon formed against you shall prosper, and every tongue which rises against you in judgment you shall condemn" (Isaiah 54:17). But sometimes you also have to break word curses demon-inspired people release at you in the midst of the battle. I was completely covered in witchcraft after the encounter I just mentioned, yet had to step into the pulpit. Two leaders of the church were savvy enough to recognize the attack and assist me in quickly breaking off the assignment.

The visiting minister, who was the initial target of the demonic attack, told me that she was experiencing head, neck and back pain from whatever assignment the wild-eyed, demonized woman had unleashed against her. We also broke that assignment off in the name of Jesus and the pain left.

After leaving the service for some time, the Jezebelic woman returned to the sanctuary and started releasing word curses against me as I preached. One leader actually saw fiery darts from the spiritual realm coming against me. We had asked intercessors to be positioned around the sanctuary to combat any onslaught, and I continued to give my message unaffected.

Remember, no weapon formed against you can prosper. But that does not mean you ignore the fiery darts flying toward you. And it does not mean you wrestle solo.

Resistance to the Move of God

God prevailed as I persevered: "He who is in you is greater than he who is in the world" (1 John 4:4). I delivered a prophetic message despite the warfare. The enemy created a disturbance in hopes of robbing people in the room of their faith to receive the message. And, truth be known, the demonized person's attacks did scare some in the congregation who had never seen an outpouring of the Spirit of God, much less demonic resistance to it.

The spirit of religion works to quench God's power—and Jezebel works to cut off the prophetic voice. Religion and Jezebel both partner with witchcraft to get the job done.

Let's look at this in Scripture. Paul warned Timothy that in the last days perilous times would come. His list of characteristics evident in those days describes an environment that is ripe for demonic manifestations:

> But know this, that in the last days perilous times will come: For men will be lovers of themselves, lovers of money, boasters, proud, blasphemers, disobedient to parents, unthankful, unholy, unloving, unforgiving, slanderers, without self-control, brutal, despisers of good, traitors, headstrong, haughty, lovers of pleasure rather than lovers of God, having a form of godliness but denying its power. And from such people turn away!
>
> 2 Timothy 3:1–5

Can you see the idolatry in this list: *lovers of themselves, lovers of money, unforgiving, without self-control, unholy, lovers of pleasure rather than lovers of God?* The spirit of Jezebel works to woo God's people into immorality and idolatry (see Revelation 2:20). There are also open doors for witchcraft in this list: *disobedient, slanderers, headstrong.* The spirit of religion is also in the mix (think how this was manifested in the Pharisees): *unloving, traitors, having a form of godliness but denying its power.*

As we will discover further in upcoming chapters, the religious spirit has no love for you. People with a religious spirit put heavy burdens on others (see Matthew 23:4). They like to boast in their knowledge and accomplishments (see Matthew 23:5–10). They neglect the weightier matters of the law: justice, mercy and faith (see Matthew 23:23). They appear righteous on the outside, but inside they are hypocrites (see Matthew 23:27–28). Jezebel and religion are both credited with killing the prophets. These spirits do not want the power of God to manifest.

But nothing is too hard for God (see Jeremiah 32:27). At the name of Jesus, every knee must bow—and during that prophetic conference every knee did. When we made the altar call, many were filled with the Spirit, many received prophetic words, and many were delivered from hurts and wounds. Indeed, many experienced a touch from God they had never experienced before. The demonized person remained present, and quiet. She chose not to participate in the altar call, but she was treated with love, kindness and forgiveness—and was offered counseling.

I tell you all that to say this: When you move in the things of the Spirit you can expect resistance. You can expect manifestations. You can expect full-blown attacks. You might not anticipate how or when—or through whom—an attack will come, but be assured that you can take authority over it in the name of Jesus, even if the demon causes a stir before it bows.

Never let any commotion distract you from what God has in mind for His people. God is there in the midst of the resistance, the manifestations and the full-blown attacks to set the captives free. Your job is to walk in love and authority and refuse to let the enemy's shenanigans rob the people God has called you to serve.

Dealing with Prophetic Witchcraft

The promise of personal prophecy always draws a crowd. Many long to hear the voice of God and either do not have confidence in their own prophetic listening skills or seek confirmation about something they think God spoke to their hearts. I remember what it was like to be a new believer when visiting prophets would roll through town. I would wait in anticipation, hoping I would be the one called out to receive a life-changing prophetic word. Although I believe wholeheartedly in personal prophecy—and although I have attended many prophetic conferences—I have had a "prophet" call me out with a word only once. It was so far off base that it cured me of chasing after personal prophecy!

Still, I get it. I understand that believers are sincerely hungry to hear God's voice. And that, unfortunately, is one of the reasons prophetic ministry is so abused in this hour. It is one of the reasons anyone who claims to be a prophet can so easily fleece some sheep or offer false prophecies that lead people away from God instead of closer to Him. (If you are interested in prophetic ministry, check out my book *The Making of a Prophet* [Chosen, 2014].)

We have discussed the motives of the Baal prophets and the Jezebel prophets and how to recognize them. But how do you deal with prophetic witchcraft? Let me tell you my personal story.

I have seen and heard of "prophecy lines" in which so-called prophets walk past the saints while humiliating them and even releasing witchcraft curses over them—in the name of Jesus. Actually, I witnessed and experienced it firsthand many years ago at a prophetic gathering that featured a pastor from another nation who was convinced God had shifted his ministry from the pastoral into the prophetic office. He had worked alongside a very accurate prophet for years and now claimed he was coming into his own prophetic ministry. God can certainly shift you into a new anointing. The problem was, not only did he lack accuracy—he was flowing in the wrong spirit.

I stood on the front row of the church for hours while the special guest prophesied over at least a hundred people, one by one. I did not hear every single word, but I heard a lot of it because he carried a microphone. What I heard turned my stomach more than once. This pastor-prophet had nothing but negative words to offer most people—words about how they needed to do this better, or do more of that, or quit doing something else.

It seems he forgot the Scripture about the simple gift of prophecy: "He who prophesies speaks edification and exhortation and comfort to men" (1 Corinthians 14:3). Nothing I heard him say edified anyone, exhorted anyone or comforted anyone. Rather, it tore down, condemned and discomforted. And, in fact, it got worse as he went along. In my case, his words came at me with spiritual force that made me feel as if I had been covered with goo. My eyes began burning. I felt as though I was in a daze. It was spiritual witchcraft. I had to find someone else to lay hands on me and break the word curses against my mind.

You might wonder why I let him pray over me. I was in a leadership position in this particular church and, as such, was expected to go up for prophetic prayer whenever it was offered. Any leaders who did not do so were rebuked later. I learned a hard lesson that day, but I am glad I learned it then because it helped me move forward.

Since we are spirit beings created in the image of God, our words are not just sounds or vibrations—our words are spirit (see John 6:63). Spiritual witchcraft sometimes manifests in prophetic ministry that is impure, immature or presumptuous.

Witchcraft can tap in to the death-and-life-producing power of the tongue, which James called "a fire, a world of iniquity" (see James 3:6). James also called the tongue "an unruly evil, full of deadly poison" (see James 3:8). Witchcraft relies on the fact that death and life are in power of the tongue—ours and other people's—to release its attacks.

When Prophecy Releases Witchcraft

And that is just what happened. I was not the only one who left the prayer line covered with goo, with burning eyes and otherwise dazed and confused. Several individuals came up to me asking about the harsh words they had received. Some dismissed it as poor prophecy, but others were hurt.

When a prophet leaves a cloud of false prophecy behind as he or she heads off to the next city on the itinerary, it is important that we handle the aftermath with maturity. I helped some people work through those issues by dismissing the poor prophecy and breaking the words over them in the name of Jesus. Others helped me deal with the witchcraft-laced words spoken over me by binding them in the name of Jesus and pleading the blood of Jesus over me—and speaking over me the opposite of the false prophetic words.

When the issue of the poor and hurtful prophetic utterances was brought to the leadership of the church, those who questioned this pastor-prophet's ministry were sorely rebuked by those leaders flowing in a spirit of religion. After all, who were we to question this great man of God with an international ministry? How could we suggest that even a single word that came out of his mouth fell to the ground?

That is idolatrous religion. And that was probably the saddest part of all. Even the most accurate, mature prophet can miss it.

As Spirit-filled believers we have the right and responsibility to judge prophetic words over our lives. We should embrace the true prophetic words and dismiss—and even break the power of—words that are not from God. The paradigm that sets prophets on a pedestal, not to be questioned, must end.

Overcoming Witchcraft Attacks

I have offered in this chapter two scenarios that illustrate how Jezebel, religion and witchcraft work together to release spiritual warfare against you through curses. But you do not have to be speaking at an event or receiving a prophetic word in a prayer line in order to be hit with witchcraft. And it does not have to be Halloween or Lent for a witchcraft attack to come against your mind and body. Your co-worker can release a word curse against you. Your mate can speak words of death over you. And you can do a fine job of cursing yourself.

So how do you prevent—and if not prevent then overcome—these attacks? Let's get practical.

1. Gird the Loins of Your Mind

The first step in any battle is to be mentally prepared. In the words of Scripture: "Gird up the loins of your mind, be sober, and rest your hope fully upon the grace that is to be brought to you at the revelation of Jesus Christ" (1 Peter 1:13).

If we are mentally and spiritually alert, we can reject the enemy's plan to dig a spiritual ditch that is hard to climb out of. Paul warns us not to allow the enemy to take advantage of us (see 2 Corinthians 2:11). That means we cannot ignore the devil or underestimate his craftiness. Peter tells us: "Be sober, be vigilant; because your adversary the devil walks about like a roaring lion, seeking whom he may devour. Resist him, steadfast in the faith, knowing that the same sufferings are experienced by your brotherhood in the world" (1 Peter 5:8–9).

There can be a fine line between being aware of our enemy and being overly focused on him, but it is not difficult to stay in bounds if we gird up the loins of our minds.

The Reformation Study Bible offers this commentary on 1 Peter 1:13, which gives practical insight into the process: "As we would say, 'fasten your belt' or 'roll up your sleeves.' Peter asks us to prepare for vigorous and sustained spiritual exertion."

Girding up the loins of our mind is work. *The Message* translation says, "Put your mind in gear," and *The Amplified Bible* says, "Brace up your minds; be sober (circumspect, morally alert)." This is not a passive stance!

See, the battle really is in the mind—or at least it starts there. I remember when a friend of mine, James, who had had a stroke many years before, began manifesting post-stroke symptoms out of the blue. He started getting dizzy and his eye began twitching just as it had right after the stroke. He had headaches. He was telling people how these were the same symptoms he had experienced after his stroke. He began to consider pulling back from what God was calling him to do.

The enemy was working overtime on his mind, trying to convince him that the post-stroke medical conditions from which God had delivered him were returning. He was voicing some level of agreement with the symptoms—what many in the modern healing movement call "lying vanities" (see Jonah 2:8 KJV). When I recognized what was happening, I exposed the enemy's plan, and we prayed in agreement to break the witchcraft. He renounced any ties to his "old man"—pre-Jesus he had been a heroin addict—and the lying vanities disappeared.

During the same season—actually at the same time my friend was experiencing post-stroke symptoms—a lump manifested on the back of my neck. It itched and burned like fire. Then I had ear pain so bad I could hardly think, "knives" in my throat when I swallowed and "rocks" in my stomach—all at once. I stood against the witchcraft in the name of Jesus, but my imagination was running wild.

After days of increasingly worse symptoms that nearly debilitated me, I finally broke down and went to the doctor. My vitals were normal. No sign of infection. I had to gird up the loins of my mind and dig into the Word, speaking it over my life and breaking all agreement with the enemy, before the symptoms all fled. Sometimes you just have to dig deeper.

2. Guard Your Heart

While we are girding our minds—our souls—we also have to guard our hearts—our spirits. Look at Proverbs 4:23: "Keep your heart with all diligence, for out of it spring the issues of life." We have to guard our hearts when we are under attack because the temptation is to look for a way of escape. Our thoughts take up the cause and lead us to take actions.

Be assured that the spirit of witchcraft is not going to lead you to worship Jesus, read your Bible or pray. In fact, you might feel like doing just the opposite. Jezebel and her witchcrafts work to draw you into sin.

Remember, Jezebel works to seduce you into idolatry or immorality—and one of the weapons it uses to woo you is witchcraft. When you are under heavy attack, your heart gets weary by satanic design. Daniel notes Satan's strategy to "wear out the saints of the most High" (Daniel 7:25 kjv). This dual attack on your heart and mind is the reason Jesus said, "Come to Me, all you who labor and are heavy laden, and I will give you rest. Take My yoke upon you and learn from Me, for I am gentle and lowly in heart, and you will find rest for your souls. For My yoke is easy and My burden is light" (Matthew 11:28–30).

When you feel an oppressive yoke or burden upon you, it could be witchcraft. Jesus can offer rest to you, if you run to Him. Jezebel wants to provide you a different way of escape through sin. Jezebel may entice you into sexual sin for a momentary escape. Jezebel may tempt you with drugs or alcohol or something else that is ungodly. You may be thinking, *I would never fall for that.* I pray you never would, but please: When you feel as though you are getting hit from every side, guard your heart.

Never be too proud to think you cannot fall: "Pride goes before destruction, and a haughty spirit before a fall" (Proverbs 16:18). What is more, Paul warns this:

> Therefore let him who thinks he stands take heed lest he fall. No temptation has overtaken you except such as is common to man; but God is faithful, who will not allow you to be tempted beyond what you are able, but with the temptation will also make the way of escape, that you may be able to bear it.
>
> 1 Corinthians 10:12–13

Again, we have to guard our hearts when we are under attack, because our human response is to look for a way of escape. The Preacher said:

> Keep your heart with all diligence, for out of it spring the issues of life. Put away from you a deceitful mouth, and put perverse lips far from you. Let your eyes look straight ahead, and your eyelids look right before you. Ponder the path of your feet, and let all your ways be established. Do not turn to the right or the left; remove your foot from evil.
>
> Proverbs 4:23–27

Do not run into temptation when you are under attack. Run for cover—run to Jesus. He always causes us to triumph! (See 2 Corinthians 2:14.)

3. Cast Down Imaginations

Imaginations do not always push sickness on you or tempt you to sin. Sometimes the devil just wants to overwhelm you with witchcraft imaginations so you will give up and go hide in a cave with a big bowl of ice cream, a pillow and the TV remote control. This may not seem like such a bad thing. We all need downtime, right? We all need rest in Christ, yes, but we also do not want to lie down in a sugar coma and waste time.

Look at these words from the apostle Paul:

See then that you walk circumspectly, not as fools but as wise, redeeming the time, because the days are evil. Therefore do not be unwise, but understand what the will of the Lord is. And do not be drunk with wine, in which is dissipation; but be filled with the Spirit, speaking to one another in psalms and hymns and spiritual songs, singing and making melody in your heart to the Lord.

Ephesians 5:15–19

Can you see the contrast?

If the Holy Spirit dwells in you, then so does the fruit of self-control. But witchcraft attacks cause you to want to give up, to give in, to lie down and to "veg out." It starts with the mind. The goal is to gird the loins of our minds so that witchcraft imaginations cannot enter our thought lives in the first place. But sometimes the enemy catches us off guard. When witchcraft imaginations enter our minds and start influencing our emotions and will, we need to move quickly to combat the enemy fire. Remember, we are in a war—but we are not wrestling against flesh and blood, but against principalities, powers, the rulers of the darkness of this age and spiritual hosts of wickedness in the heavenly places (see Ephesians 6:12).

Two of those enemies are Jezebel and witchcraft. Thank God, He has equipped us with powerful weapons to overcome. Paul explains:

> For though we walk in the flesh, we do not war after the flesh: (For the weapons of our warfare are not carnal, but mighty through God to the pulling down of strong holds;) casting down imaginations, and every high thing that exalteth itself against the knowledge of God, and bringing into captivity every thought to the obedience of Christ; and having in a readiness to revenge all disobedience, when your obedience is fulfilled.
>
> 2 Corinthians 10:3–6 KJV

We can pull down strongholds that Jezebel and her witchcrafts—or any other spiritual enemy—have erected in our minds with our spiritual weapons. Paul does not tell us what those spiritual weapons are in this passage, but they would certainly include truth, righteousness, peace, the shield of faith (which makes it possible to stop the enemy's fiery darts), the helmet of salvation and the sword of the Spirit, which is the Word of God, and prayer (see Ephesians 6:14–18).

God has endowed us with the power that raised Christ from the dead (see Romans 8:11). He has given us the authority in His name to cast out demons and much more (see Mark 16:17–18).

Clearly, we are warring from a position of victory. But we have to choose by our will to wield those weapons. Witchcraft works to discourage us so we will leave our armor in the closet and lay our weapons down while the enemy floods our imaginations with sinful thoughts and desires, self-condemnation, and questions about God's will for our lives—or even His love toward us.

God has given us His Word and wisdom to discern when the thoughts rolling around in our heads fail to line up with that truth. It is up to us to cast down the imaginations and replace them with the opposite thought in line with Scripture. Nobody can cast down those scary, hurtful or otherwise wrong thoughts for you—and nobody can replace them but you. Even if you cannot find a Scripture that is specifically the opposite of the demonic thought, you can still follow Paul's advice:

> Finally, brethren, whatever things are true, whatever things are noble, whatever things are just, whatever things are pure, whatever things are lovely, whatever things are of good report, if there is any virtue and if there is anything praiseworthy— meditate on these things. The things which you learned and received and heard and saw in me, these do, and the God of peace will be with you.
>
> Philippians 4:8–9

You can do it!

4. Cast Your Cares on the Lord

I am not saying you do not have legitimate problems or concerns. I know all about legitimate problems and concerns— and they tend to come in floods overwhelming us at times. But mature spiritual warriors understand the balance between taking responsibility and casting your cares on the Lord. God will not do our part, and we cannot do His part. Apart from Him we can do nothing (see John 15:5). But through Christ who gives us strength, we can do all things (see Philippians 4:13).

Peter wrote that we should cast all our cares on the Lord, because He cares for us (see 1 Peter 5:7). He probably got the notion from David, who said: "Cast your burden on the LORD, and He shall sustain you; He shall never permit the righteous to be moved" (Psalm 55:22). There you have two witnesses! You may be thinking, *That's all well and good, but how do I actually cast my care on the Lord?* The first step is to stop wrestling the enemy in your own strength.

Again, apart from Him we can do nothing, but through Christ who gives us strength we can do all things. Trust in God is part of the foundation of successful warfare. When we hold on to our care, we are not trusting God as our Provider, the Holy Spirit as our Helper or Jesus as our Peace. The hustle and bustle and circumstantial chaos have won our attention. We cannot blame that on the devil because God clearly tells us to keep our eyes on Him. We need to pray for a greater revelation of the grace of God. We need to meditate on Scriptures about the peace of God. And we need to rely on one another to pray for us when we are so stressed out we cannot verbalize a petition.

Never be too proud to ask for prayer. And never be too proud to pray. It is through prayer that we cast our cares on the Lord: "Be anxious for nothing, but in everything by prayer and supplication, with thanksgiving, let your requests be made known to God; and the peace of God, which surpasses all understanding, will guard your hearts and minds through Christ Jesus" (Philippians 4:6–7).

Witchcraft imaginations skew your perspective—making monumental issues out of something God could fix with a wink. Cast your care on the Lord. Keep your eyes on Him. Pray for what you think you need—then believe He has you covered. When you do, He promises to care for you and give you perfect peace (see Isaiah 26:3).

5. *Speak the Word*

You have three powerful weapons at your disposal—spiritual weapons that are mighty through God to pull down strongholds: the Word, the name and the blood. It is hard to wield those weapons effectively when you are wallowing in condemnation, self-pity, fear or some other harmful emotion.

Get the Word of God in your mouth because it is your spiritual sword (see Ephesians 6:17). Remember, "the word of God is living and powerful, and sharper than any two-edged sword, piercing even to the division of soul and spirit, and of joints and marrow, and is a discerner of the thoughts and intents of the heart" (Hebrews 4:12).

When you speak the Word out loud, you are releasing the power of life over yourself (see Proverbs 18:21). When you speak the Word out loud—or even think about it—you are transforming your thoughts by the renewing of your mind (see Romans 12:2). God's Word carries creative power (see Genesis 1). Speaking God's Word can move mountains (see Mark 11:23). Angels also heed the voice of God's Word (see Psalm 103:20) to help us in warfare.

Speak the Word to your problems, because the Word of God always accomplishes its purpose. The Lord Himself promises: "So shall My word be that goes forth from My mouth; it shall not return to Me void, but it shall accomplish what I please, and it shall prosper in the thing for which I sent it" (Isaiah 55:11).

6. *Use the Name of Jesus*

We must use the name of Jesus, because that is where our authority lies. Jesus gave us permission to use His name—the name above all names. At the name of Jesus every knee has to bow. That means every knee in heaven, every knee on earth, every knee under the earth (see Philippians 2:10). And every knee includes Jezebel, religion and witchcraft.

Now, that does not mean you will pull down demonic strongholds once and for all, never having to wrestle with them again. Until Jesus returns, the devil has a right to roam this earth like a roaring lion looking for someone to devour (see 1 Peter 5:8)—and so do his principalities and powers and the rest of his demonic hierarchy. But in our spiritual battles the devil has to bow to the name of Jesus, when we are fully submitted to Him.

Many times it seems we pray and the devil does not flee. That may be because we have some common ground with the enemy. Keep in mind that the Bible does not only say resist the devil and he will flee. The Bible actually says much more:

> He gives more grace. Therefore He says: "God resists the proud, but gives grace to the humble." Therefore submit to God. Resist the devil and he will flee from you. Draw near to God and He will draw near to you. Cleanse your hands, you sinners; and purify your hearts, you double-minded.
>
> James 4:6–8

Is that not a far cry from what some spiritual warfare circles teach? See, we can have pride in our spiritual warfare skills. That pride can cause us to stumble before our enemies because God resists the proud and gives grace to the humble. We need the grace of God to overcome our enemies.

Flaunting our spiritual warfare skills like a boastful five-star general will most certainly lead to defeat. King Ahab was full of pride. God's prophet Micaiah told him what no other false prophet on his payroll would: that he would lose if he went to battle against Ramoth Gilead (see 1 Kings 22:17–23). Instead of heeding the voice of God's prophet, proud Ahab had him arrested and ran to the battle line. He was killed.

By the same token, you cannot toss around the name of Jesus as though it is some magic word. True and lasting victory comes through faith in the name of Jesus and intimate relationship with Him. You cannot have warfare-winning faith in a God you do not really know. In other words, our revelation of Jesus as Warrior and our submission to Him as King play a role in forcing the devil to flee.

Remember the itinerant Jewish exorcists who took it upon themselves to use the name of Jesus to cast out demons? They proclaimed,

> "We exorcise you by the Jesus whom Paul preaches." Also there were seven sons of Sceva, a Jewish chief priest, who did so. And the evil spirit answered and said, "Jesus I know, and Paul I know; but who are you?" Then the man in whom the evil spirit was leaped on them, overpowered them, and prevailed against them, so that they fled out of that house naked and wounded.
>
> Acts 19:13–16

How embarrassing!

See, they were not submitted to God, and they did not have a relationship with Jesus, so they really did not have faith in His name. God has given us victory in warfare, but we need to have our faith firmly rooted in Him before we can truly stand in our authority in Christ in the face of Jezebel and her witchcrafts. So find out who you are in Christ, stay humble and rely on His grace. Then, in faith, bind the enemy's operations in the name of Jesus, and loose the opposite of what is manifesting in your life.

7. Invoke the Blood of Jesus

When witchcraft is plaguing you, plead the blood of Jesus over your mind. You have been bought with a price—spirit, soul and body. Your soul includes your mind, will and emotions.

In Him, we have redemption through His blood (see Ephesians 1:7). Through our faith in Christ—through His shed blood—we have been delivered "from the power of darkness and conveyed . . . into the kingdom of the Son of His love" (Colossians 1:13). We overcome the devil by the blood of the Lamb and the word of our testimony (see Revelation 12:11). When you cannot think of any Scripture, plead the blood of Jesus. Here is a practical example:

"Father, I thank You for the blood of Jesus that cleanses me from all unrighteousness. I thank You for the power in the blood of Jesus unto my salvation, which includes protection and deliverance. I plead the blood of Jesus over my mind and body right now!"

8. Pray in the Spirit

Likewise, when you cannot think of any Scripture, pray in the Spirit. In Matthew 26:41, Jesus said to watch and pray. He also said that our spirits are willing but our flesh is weak. Your spirit man wants to pray. Your flesh wants to lie in bed and sleep, stuff its face full of potato chips or whine about something. Your spirit man wants to leap into intercession and work with the Holy Spirit to bring the will of God into the earth—and overcome enemy opposition. Who will win out?

When you feel heavyhearted, when you feel depressed, when you feel oppressed, when you feel out of sorts, stay clear of your carnal mind. Pray in the Spirit. The Holy Spirit is willing to help you with your infirmities, and He wants to pray through you to help the infirmities of others. Remember, the Spirit is willing but the flesh is weak. Walk after the Spirit and you will not fulfill the lusts of the flesh.

I pray in tongues for extended periods every day. I believe praying in tongues builds me up (see 1 Corinthians 14:4, 18), as I speak directly to God (see 1 Corinthians 14:2, 14). I believe praying in tongues stirs my faith (see Jude 20). I believe praying in tongues assures me that I am praying God's perfect will (see Romans 8:26–27). There are many benefits to praying in tongues. That is why I do it as much as I can, and I encourage other believers to do the same. I also believe that praying in tongues can help us combat our enemies—enemies that we might not even discern we are battling.

9. Break Word Curses

Because witchcraft can come through the deathly words others speak over us—whether we actually hear them or not— we need to break word curses. There are seasons when the Holy Spirit shows me that word curses are working against me. People can also speak word curses over our families.

I remember one time my daughter was going through some difficulties and making some errors in judgment. A Spirit-filled believer dared to speak these words: "Don't get mad at me for saying this, but your daughter is not following the Lord." That was a word curse, which we swiftly broke. She was young and making some mistakes, but she was also attending church services faithfully, ministering on missions trips and seeking God for help.

Break these curses over you and your family quickly. Otherwise, the power of death can work in the spirit against you. Simply say, "I break that word curse in the name of Jesus!"

10. Bless Those Who Curse You

After you break the word curses, bless those who curse you—whether you know who they are or not. People who curse God still receive His blessings of life, sunshine, rain and many other things they take for granted. If we want to be Christlike—and we do—then we need to bless those who curse us. Here are Jesus' words:

> "You have heard that it was said, 'You shall love your neighbor and hate your enemy.' But I say to you, love your enemies, bless those who curse you, do good to those who hate you, and pray for those who spitefully use you and persecute you, that you may be sons of your Father in heaven; for He makes His sun rise on the evil and on the good, and sends rain on the just and on the unjust. For if you love those who love you, what reward have you? Do not even the tax collectors do the same?"
>
> Matthew 5:43–46

This is not the only instance in Scripture that bears witness to this concept. Paul tells us: "Bless those who persecute you; bless and do not curse" (Romans 12:14). James writes:

> With it [the tongue] we bless our God and Father, and with it we curse men, who have been made in the similitude of God. Out of the same mouth proceed blessing and cursing. My brethren, these things ought not to be so. Does a spring send forth fresh water and bitter from the same opening?
>
> James 3:9–11

Armed with understanding of how witchcraft works, we can cast down witchcraft's curses. There is tremendous power in these fundamentals if you will apply them. The challenge is often discerning that you are under attack. That is where relationships with other mature Christians are helpful. They can often see what we cannot—and they can help us battle what is coming against us.

When you are under spiritual assault, be careful not to isolate yourself and let Jezebel beat up on you with her witchcrafts. Run for cover. Run to those of like precious faith. Run to Jesus.

7

Religion's Disarming Agenda

Religion disarmed me—but I had no idea I was stuck in religion's trap until I escaped from it. See, the problem with religious deception is that you do not know you are deceived. If you knew you were deceived, you would walk away from the lie and embrace the truth. Lovers of the truth are less likely to be deceived, but anyone can fall prey to the spirit of religion's deception because it looks so beautiful and righteous on the outside. But behind the whitewash, it is dead, unclean and full of hypocrisy and lawlessness (see Matthew 23:27–28).

Religion can disarm you in many ways; it wooed me into a performance trap. When I was born again, I looked immediately for ways to serve God in our church. (I was living in Alabama at the time.) I was willing to do anything and everything, from vacuuming floors to changing smelly diapers. It did not matter. I had a heart full of gratitude and wanted to serve. In my early days as a Christian, service was a joy. But that joy turned into drudgery when I moved to a new state and started volunteering in a very different church.

The leaders saw my heart to serve, saw my gifts and saw my talents—and took advantage of all three in the name of Jesus. I was such a young believer at the time, I had no idea that the spirit of religion used these ambitious leaders to set a trap for me and disarm me.

Publicly, they taught "God, family, ministry," but secretly they demanded, "Ministry, ministry, ministry." Our Bibles fell open to the fivefold gifting of Ephesians 4:11, and we spelled ministry *w-o-r-k*. I literally volunteered forty hours a week of my time, while also working at my job and raising a daughter as a single mother. It was out of balance, and it led to disaster.

When I look back, I can see clearly how the religious spirit, working through these leaders, was holding me in bondage through a strategic combination of rewards and recognition at certain times, and public humiliation and punishment at other times. One minute I was honored at a ministry banquet as MVP of the Year; the next minute I was being criticized for not producing enough quickly enough.

This went on for several years, until the day came when I was so burned out and facing such a crisis in my family that I told these leaders I was taking a break from the work of the ministry. When I did, they went on the attack. They told me they would have to pray about whether or not to let me continue serving in ministry ever again. They told others that I was immature, unstable and full of fear. I was on the blacklist because I pulled the plug on my performance.

When you refuse to bow to the religious spirit's demands, it seeks to crucify you. The religious scribes, Pharisees and Sadducees might not have nailed Jesus to the cross when He refused to obey their demands, but these religious leaders were indeed the ones who called for His crucifixion.

After being sorely rebuked and having my walk with God criticized, I started to question the status quo at my church.

When I did, they told me I was deceived. A week earlier I had been teaching in the church, but suddenly I was immature, unstable and full of fear—and deceived? It was part of religion's agenda to disarm believers.

When I began praying for God to break the deception over my mind, I could finally see Satan's deadly trio in operation. I knew I was being deceived; I just needed to know *how* I was being deceived. Was I wrong to question the practices of the church, or was I right to escape its abusive system? Religion had disarmed and oppressed me for years, but God delivered me in an instant when I was willing to lay down my front row seat—my titles and authority in the religious system—and seek the truth.

Just as Jesus promised, the truth made me free (see John 8:32).

Religion's Rules and Regulations

Religion is legalistic and performance-oriented—and we see this plague in too many churches today. Sincere believers who are hooked by the spirit of religion soon find that if they do not burn out from the demands, their relationships and ministries are often destroyed.

The performance trap is not a manifestation solely of overwhelming church work. By stacking up rules and regulations that you feel you must live up to in order to remain worthy of your position in Christ, the spirit of religion deceives you to believe you have been stripped of your rightful spiritual authority and your protective armor when you fail to meet its unreachable demands. Of course, religion cannot rob you of your spiritual authority or armor.

Jesus had quite a lot to say about the scribes and Pharisees, who personify the religious spirit in the New Testament. Jesus noted: "They crush you with impossible religious demands and never lift a finger to help ease the burden" (Matthew 23:4 NLT). Religion wants you at church every time the door is open—services twice a week, midweek Bible study, men's meeting, church picnic, fundraising events, conferences, leadership training, Sunday school, outreach and the list goes on—regardless of obligations to career or family.

I am all for church participation, but religion will burn you out with obligation and then condemn you for not being able to keep up. That is because the religious spirit is all about appearances. If you fail to show up at all the functions—plus do not volunteer beforehand to print and distribute the flyers, bake the cakes and otherwise organize the outings—then you become a second-class citizen.

Speaking of the Pharisees—the personification of the religious spirit—Jesus said that everything they do is for show: "They love to sit at the head table at church dinners, basking in the most prominent positions, preening in the radiance of public flattery, receiving honorary degrees, and getting called 'Doctor' and 'Reverend'" (Matthew 23:6–7 MESSAGE).

Maybe you know some church leaders who insist on being called by a title—or a string of titles—and get offended when you do not oblige. That is the religious spirit manifesting, and it will soon put a demand on you to serve its purposes, to exalt it. Jesus said, "He who is greatest among you shall be your servant. And whoever exalts himself will be humbled, and he who humbles himself will be exalted" (Matthew 23:11–12). People flowing in a religious spirit—whether they are in leadership or not—want to be exalted.

Religious Condemnation

Jesus called these religious types "serpents," and said they would receive "greater condemnation" (Matthew 23:14). The religious spirit knows its condemnation is coming. This has been prophesied repeatedly. I believe that is why this spirit works so hard to heap condemnation on us when we will not bow to its agenda. Religious condemnation works to disarm us by trying to strip us of our identity in Christ by demanding we follow rules and regulations perfectly in order to receive the love of God, the grace of God, the approval of God, the blessing of God, the acceptance of God—in order to remain in right standing with God.

Paul explained that we receive the righteousness of God through faith in Jesus Christ:

> For all have sinned and fall short of the glory of God, being justified freely by His grace through the redemption that is in Christ Jesus, whom God set forth as a propitiation by His blood, through faith, to demonstrate His righteousness, because in His forbearance God had passed over the sins that were previously committed, to demonstrate at the present time His righteousness, that He might be just and the justifier of the one who has faith in Jesus.
>
> Romans 3:23–26

The spirit of religion sets us up to fail. Works do not save us—and we do not earn God's love, grace, approval, blessing or acceptance through them. Works that aim to win God's favor are part of the religious spirit's system to keep us in bondage. We are God's workmanship, and we were created in Christ Jesus to do good works that God has prepared for us (see Ephesians 2:10)—but we do not earn God's grace through doing them. There is a big difference. Religion blurs the line to keep us under its thumb—and under condemnation when we cannot measure up.

That does not mean we have a license to sin. It means we have a license to approach the throne of grace boldly when we sin, to find grace and mercy and forgiveness (see Hebrews 4:16). The apostle John put it this way:

> If we walk in the light as He is in the light, we have fellowship with one another, and the blood of Jesus Christ His Son cleanses us from all sin. If we say that we have no sin, we deceive ourselves, and the truth is not in us. If we confess our sins, He is faithful and just to forgive us our sins and to cleanse us from all unrighteousness. If we say that we have not sinned, we make Him a liar, and His word is not in us.
>
> 1 John 1:7–10

Laying Down Your Weapons

The religious spirit carries a double-edged sword that usually divides its victims into two camps: the powerless and the self-righteous. The powerless wind up wallowing in self-condemnation, too beaten down to fight the spiritual attack against their minds. The self-righteous wind up in spiritual pride, judging and further burdening others who cannot meet the standards they themselves achieve. Either way, religion's victims are set up for a fall. Let's look first at the camp of the "powerless."

I stated above that the religious spirit cannot remove the protective armor of God from you (see Ephesians 6:10–11). It can, however, deceive you into thinking you are not worthy of using it, and attacks your mind toward that end.

Since the religious spirit has no right to unbuckle your belt of truth, it works with spiritual witchcraft to bombard your mind with imaginations that exalt its lies above God's truth. If you start down the path of guilt and condemnation, you will be less likely to discern the witchcraft attack against your mind. You will, more likely, begin meditating on the negative thoughts about yourself and your circumstances—and other people—that the enemy whispers. You might shift your focus from criticism of yourself to criticism of others.

At this point, you are no longer thinking of things that are true. You have laid down a vital element of your armor, and the enemy is setting you up for greater deception.

You can combat this, as we discussed in an earlier chapter, by "casting down arguments and every high thing that exalts itself against the knowledge of God, bringing every thought into captivity to the obedience of Christ" (2 Corinthians 10:5).

The belt of truth is not the only piece of armor the religious spirit is after. This devil is also targeting your breastplate of righteousness. Remember, the religious spirit is after your identity in Christ. This enemy knows that if you begin questioning your right standing with God, even for a minute, you will not dare to pick up the sword of the Spirit and wield it against the deceiving religious spirit—or against witchcraft or Jezebel.

Scripture says, "If God is for us, who can be against us?" (Romans 8:31). But the religious spirit will work with witchcraft to flood your mind with thoughts that God is angry with you. Those condemning thoughts cause you to run away from God, rather than to God. If you sin, God is not happy with your behavior, but He still loves you and is waiting to restore fellowship with you. All you have to do is repent and keep moving in God.

The religious spirit's condemnation tries to get believers to trade our Jesus-given peace for devil-inspired worry, turmoil and all manner of upset. Paul taught that we have shoes of peace. But when religious condemnation attacks our minds, we soon kick off those shoes and kick ourselves in the fanny instead. In other words, instead of being at peace knowing that we can ask God for forgiveness—and that He indeed will forgive us—we beat ourselves up in twisted penance until we think we have paid enough to receive what the blood of Christ freely offers: another chance.

Paul said, above all, to keep the shield of faith held high so you can quench all the fiery darts of the wicked one (see Ephesians 6:16). But it is hard to muster faith in a God you feel is mad at you. With the shield of faith lost somewhere in the closet of condemnation, the enemy sets up camp in your mind. Witchcraft then shoots fiery darts, like machine-gun fire in the spirit, and your faith goes up in flames. You have the helmet of salvation, but the enemy's witchcraft imaginations can leave you feeling so condemned that you question your salvation.

When this happens, you are no longer submitting yourself to God or resisting the devil. And the religious devils that have you in bondage to self-condemnation do not plan on fleeing.

If the attack against you gets to this point, you need to reach out to friends or family who can help you break the witchcraft off your mind. Pick up the sword of the Spirit immediately. If you cannot do anything more than hold your Bible and read it out loud, do it—and do not stop until you get hold of your mind. Merely speaking God's Word out of your mouth will help you gird up the loins of your mind and enable the Holy Spirit to break in and speak to your heart with truth that will set you free.

Religion Keeps Records

The spirit of religion wants you to beat yourself bloody whenever you sin, and then wallow in condemnation for weeks or even months. The spirit of religion's job is to disarm you so that other spiritual foes, including Jezebel with her witch-crafts, can oppress you. But the Bible says:

> There is therefore now no condemnation to those who are in Christ Jesus, who do not walk according to the flesh, but according to the Spirit. For the law of the Spirit of life in Christ Jesus has made me free from the law of sin and death. For what the law could not do in that it was weak through the flesh, God did by sending His own Son in the likeness of sinful flesh, on account of sin: He condemned sin in the flesh, that the righteous requirement of the law might be fulfilled in us who do not walk according to the flesh but according to the Spirit.
>
> Romans 8:1–4

Learn to recognize and avoid condemnation-heaping religious antagonists who refuse to let people forget past mistakes. Once you have repented, God chooses not to remember your sins anymore (see Jeremiah 31:34). But the religious spirit remembers—and the religious spirit likes to throw past sin up in your face at convenient times to hold you back, put you down or otherwise control you.

People flowing in a religious spirit hold you in the past—to who you were yesterday; they will not let you get past your past mistakes. These Pharisees remind you of who you used to be despite clear evidence of the breakthrough work God has done in your life. While God chooses not to recall the sins for which you repent, religious bullies remind you every time you try to move forward. These are the same ones who—in order to cover their own sins—spread rumors about people who see the light and leave their churches.

I wonder how many people have given up on fellowshipping in a church because religious oppressors remind them of their past failures. And I wonder how much momentum the Body of Christ has lost because religious bullies focus more on tithing (yes, even your birthday money) while ignoring the most important aspects of the law—justice, mercy and faith (see Matthew 23:23). Yes, we should tithe and give offerings, but not while neglecting love.

Religious bullies might run in the "right" circles, dress the "right" way and say the "right" things, but inside they are filthy, full of greed and self-indulgence (see Matthew 23:25)! Jesus also called these Pharisees hypocrites: "For you are like whitewashed tombs, which indeed appear beautiful outwardly, but inside are full of dead men's bones and all uncleanness. Even so you also outwardly appear righteous to men, but inside you are full of hypocrisy and lawlessness" (Matthew 23:27–28).

We see, then, that the religious spirit's attack on the mind leaves the first camp of victims beaten down and struggling to survive. In the other camp, which we will explore now, believers allow themselves to be lifted into self-righteousness and pride—which is equally disastrous.

Spiritual Pride Blinds You

We have exposed one side of the double-edged sword—condemnation. Now let's look at the other side, which cuts just as deeply into our spiritual health. It is called spiritual pride, and it sets us up for a fleshly fall.

If you are beating yourself up for not achieving the religious spirit's standards, you know it. You feel miserable. The other side of religion's influence, however, is harder for the one trapped in its clutches to discern: spiritual pride. It is difficult for us to recognize our own spiritual pride because pride has blind spots.

Think about it. Jesus called the self-righteous, spiritually proud Pharisees "blind men" (Matthew 23:19). But they could not see it. They could see the specks in their brothers' eyes clearly, but they could not discern the log of self-righteous judgment in their own eyes. Consider this passage:

> Jesus said, "For judgment I have come into this world, that those who do not see may see, and that those who see may be made blind." Then some of the Pharisees who were with Him heard these words, and said to Him, "Are we blind also?" Jesus said to them, "If you were blind, you would have no sin; but now you say, 'We see.' Therefore your sin remains."
>
> John 9:39–41

Jesus was calling out their spiritual pride. But even with a direct word from God—face-to-face—they still could not see it. They were blind and also spiritually deaf to the words of God. Spiritual pride blinds your eyes and stops up your spiritual ears so that you cannot hear the truth. Jesus called these Pharisees "blind leaders of the blind. And if the blind leads the blind, both will fall into a ditch" (Matthew 15:14).

Have you ever wondered how some spiritual leaders fall into extreme theological ditches? Often, spiritual pride is at the root. They bought in to a theology that puffed them up and then amassed a following of people looking to reach the same spiritual heights. That is the blind leading the blind—and that is one reason why some churches are in the ditch of extremism. But the Good News is that Jesus came to heal the blind—both the naturally and spiritually blind. We just have to be humble enough to receive an eye-opening experience.

Religion Tells You Sin Is Okay

Over the years, I have run into a number of people who steadfastly believe that their strong anointing or their spiritual gifts make up for their lack of character—or even their persistent sin. In other words, they think that God accepts their behavior because He continues to use them to deliver prophetic words, heal people or otherwise administrate the flow of the Holy Spirit.

I will never forget Mark. When he preached, the anointing at the altar was strong. Words of wisdom flowed. People got healed. More than once, we saw a genuine outpouring. The Holy Spirit's manifest presence was undeniable. God was using Mark to set the captives free.

But Mark was not free—and he would not admit it. Mark had a religious spirit. He was like one of the Sons of Thunder who wanted to call fire down from heaven to consume the people who rejected Jesus (Luke 9:54). He threatened frequently to rebuke those who did not live up to his standards. He had dreams and visions of people dying because they would not come to church. His behavior was controlling, impatient and self-righteous.

When Mark's co-laborers confronted him, he suggested they were the problem. He said they were not living on the edge in faith, as he was; that they were not sold out to God, as he was; that they were not fasting and praying enough, as he was; that they just were not holy enough, as he was. So he cut off relationship with those co-laborers and took his spiritual gifts somewhere else. And that is sad because the gifts followed him out the door—but so did his ugly character flaws that could ultimately hold him back from his prophetic destiny.

Mark is not the only one I have run into who had a powerful anointing and especially poor character. And he is not the only one I have run into who justified that poor behavior through a powerful anointing.

This is another example of how the spirit of Jezebel and the spirit of religion work together to convince people that, because they can prophesy an accurate word at church, God does not mind their angry outbursts at home. Or because people are slain in the Spirit when they lay hands on them, God is pleased with the way they treat their friends. Or because a gift of healing is present, God is giving them a pass on that drinking problem, sexual sin or whatever else is hidden behind closed doors.

No, we do not have to be perfect to prophesy a perfectly accurate word. We do not have to have flawless character to minister at the altar. We do not need to be absolutely sinless to lay hands on the sick and see them recover. In fact, to suggest so would be to reflect the religious spirit, because we all have sins of omission; there is always more light to walk in.

So, what am I saying? We need to stop confusing gifts and callings with maturity and character. God can use a stubborn mule to prophesy, and He can use a stubborn believer to prophesy, too. God does not endorse stubbornness, which is like the sin of idolatry (see 1 Samuel 15:23), but if He needs a vessel to deliver a prophetic word to a person who needs desperately to hear it, He can find one. That prophetic word—or powerful altar call or gifts of healings or working of miracles—is not about puffing up or glorifying the vessel; it is about glorifying God and edifying His Church.

Religion Wants to Earn Spiritual Gifts

Good character does not earn spiritual gifts and anointing, and poor character does not remove them, at least not overnight. The Holy Spirit distributes the nine spiritual gifts— word of wisdom, word of knowledge, gift of faith, gifts of healings, working of miracles, prophecy, discerning of spirits, different kinds of tongues and interpretation of tongues—to people as He wills (see 1 Corinthians 12:4–11). It has nothing to do with our will; nor does it validate our character.

Paul wrote, "The gifts and the calling of God are irrevocable" (Romans 11:29). The Greek word for *gifts* in this verse is *charisma*, which means "a gift of grace, a gift involving grace" on the part of God as the donor. This verse is often applied to God's free grace to sinners, but I believe it can also apply to spiritual gifts and ministry callings.

If God called you into ministry, He is not going to revoke that call or the gifts that go with it the first time (or even necessarily the tenth or twentieth time) you sin. God is so slow to anger and abounding in mercy (see Numbers 14:18) that it may seem as though we are getting away with our poor behavior and behind-the-scenes sin. God is just giving us space to repent— even as He gave King Ahab and Queen Jezebel time to repent.

Repenting of Spiritual Pride

After the prophetic showdown on Mount Carmel between Elijah and the false prophets, as we have noted, Ahab went back and told Jezebel what happened. The wicked monarchs should have fallen to their knees right then and there. They did not, but they did not lose the kingdom just then, either. The gifts and callings were still there.

Look again at the chronology in this light. Ahab should have recognized the mercy of God in operation—and that he was merely a vessel God was using to bring His will to Israel. But prideful Ahab missed the mark and allowed Jezebel to frame the innocent Naboth. Only then did Elijah deliver a word of condemnation to Ahab. Ahab refused to heed the word.

God gave Ahab yet another way out, sending Micaiah the prophet to warn him. Prideful Ahab would not listen—and was killed in battle. Soon Jehu would rise up and destroy Jezebel and their entire family. But our long-suffering God gave them plenty of warnings before that happened.

I believe God is giving warnings to many spiritually gifted people with character issues and private sin in this hour. Sometimes He sends people to confront them in love about their behavior. Other times He shows them through His Word. Still other times the conviction of the Holy Spirit comes. If the Holy Spirit has shown you that Jezebel and religion have tricked you into thinking of yourself more highly than you ought—or if religion and witchcraft have you wallowing in a pit of self-condemnation so that you are failing to rise up into your calling—just repent. Turn it around. God loves you. He will deliver you from religion's agenda to disarm you and to destroy your destiny.

In his classic book *Humility*, Andrew Murray wrote:

> Humility is perfect quietness of heart. It is to expect nothing, to wonder at nothing that is done to me, to feel nothing done against me. It is to be at rest when nobody praises me, and when I am blamed or despised. It is to have a blessed home in the Lord, where I can go in and shut the door, and kneel to my Father in secret, and am at peace as in a deep sea of calmness, when all around and above is trouble.

I pray that all of us learn to discern God's loving correction in our lives, because when we ignore Him over and over and over and over and over again, we wind up deceiving ourselves (see James 1:22)—and we think that because we are anointed and prophesying accurately, God is pleased with what we do when we are not in the spotlight.

God's grace to grow up is available to us all. Our part is to meditate on His Word, set our hearts to obey and thank God for the grace to do it.

8

Embracing the
Spirit of Liberty

When I was a child, I knew about Jesus because my great-grandmother had a painting of the Last Supper over her little square dining table in her little kitchen. I used to sit there and stare at it while I ate my generic Pop-Tarts, the kind without the sugary frosting. My great-grandmother also had a portrait of Jesus in the hallway. His eyes seemed to follow me when I walked by. At the time, it seemed kind of creepy. Everywhere I went in her house, it seemed as if Jesus was right there. And He was. But because I did not know Him it made me uncomfortable. I was sort of scared of this Jesus.

When I got a little older, I lived next door to a churchgoing couple. That is to say, they were very religious on Easter and Christmas and had some religious symbols around the house, but the rest of the year they looked like any other worldly family. They happened to be Catholics, but the same could undoubtedly have been said of many Protestants. This particular couple argued a lot, cussed just as much, ate too much, drank even more and eventually got divorced. Whoever this Jesus was, while honored on holidays and depicted in little statues around their home, He seemed to be ineffective. Needless to say, I was not too impressed with their Jesus.

By the time I entered college, Jesus was not on my mind. I just knew, somehow, that I needed to "get saved" at some point in my life, but figured I would wait until I had had my fun and started living right—maybe some time in my forties. After all, I had heard that Jesus was longsuffering, so He would be there when I was ready.

Now, that was true in one sense—He is longsuffering—but the decision to "put off" embracing Christ's liberty left me in bondage to the world. For about fifteen years, I engaged in all manner of wickedness. All the while, the Jesus that was in my great-grandmother's home was watching. I had to hit a wall and hit it hard before I realized that Jesus was not the lifeless form in my Catholic neighbor's living room.

But even after I got saved, I did not have a right perception of Jesus. I merely had a skewed picture of Jesus that religion had painted for me during the first thirty years of my life.

This was largely because the spirit of religion works to pervert our perception of who Jesus is and who we are in Him. Arming myself with understanding—and revelation— of who Jesus is, what He died to give me and my identity in Him helped me resist the spirit of religion, embrace the spirit of liberty and walk in my God-given authority. God is no respecter of persons. He will give you the same understanding and revelation if you seek it.

How Do You See Jesus?

Who is Jesus to you—and what does He want from you? Stop and think about that for a minute. Really think about it. Put the book down and pick it up again after you have a clear idea of how you truly perceive Jesus, so that the truth in the rest of this chapter can truly set you free. If you think you see God rightly and you do not, you are hindering your ability to walk in your destiny. So, please, don't gloss over this. Really ask the Holy Spirit to show you if you are not seeing Him rightly.

Many people have a wrong perception of God, and it opens the door for Jezebel, witchcraft and religion to war against them. That warfare clouds their minds with witchcraft and shuts the door to the spirit of liberty that would set them free to pursue their high calling in Christ. Some people think that God is mad at them unless they are nearly perfect. That is the work of the religious spirit. Others think Jesus is okay with their unrepentant sin because He is full of mercy and grace. That is the work of the Jezebel spirit. Remember, God does not expect us to be perfect, but He does not smile on our sin, either.

Still others think God does not love them as much as He loves their neighbor or that He cannot be fully trusted or that He put sickness on them to teach them a lesson or that He is too busy to get involved in their everyday lives—or something else that the spirits of religion or Jezebel taught them. Indeed, there are many wrong perceptions about God that hinder our relationship with Him and lead us into the clutches of lifeless religion and immoral Jezebel spirits.

Understanding the Father's Heart

Jesus was an expression of the Father's heart. Jesus spent three years on earth, in part, to reveal the personality of the Father. When Jesus was raising the dead, healing the sick, cleansing the lepers, feeding the masses, providing finances, befriending sinners, extending forgiveness, teaching the Word and working various other miracles, He was mirroring the kind intentions of His Father's heart toward us.

Given over to the religious spirit, the Pharisees of Jesus' day wanted Him crucified. Much the same, the legalistic Pharisees of our day want all those who embrace the freedom found in Christ crucified. But when you know the Father's heart, you can resist the spirits of religion and Jezebel that aim to take you away from that safe place.

Too many believe that the Father is stern and hard—and just waiting for an opportunity to sideline us or even banish us from the Kingdom. This harsh concept of God the Father is damaging to our souls.

So what does the Father heart of God look like? Jesus told Thomas that anyone who has seen Him has seen the Father (see John 14:5–9). In other words, it is in the Father's heart to raise the dead, heal the sick, cleanse the lepers, feed the masses, provide finances, befriend sinners, extend forgiveness, teach the Word and work various other miracles. God the Father does not love you any less than Jesus loves you. In fact, He loves you just as He loves Jesus (see John 17:23). Meditate on that. It is a powerful truth that will propel you into greater intimacy with God.

Without intimacy with God, you cannot fulfill His perfect plan for your life no matter what you are called to do. Intimacy with God strengthens your spirit. Intimacy with God refreshes the weary soul. Intimacy with God protects you from temptation. Intimacy with God anchors your emotions. Intimacy with God builds trust. Intimacy with God is fundamental and vital for every believer.

The religious spirit wants to rob you of this godly intimacy; the Jezebel spirit wants you to get intimate with sin.

Looking into a Supernatural Mirror

Did you know that about 17 percent of Americans believe the Bible is full of man-written fables and fairy tales? Only 30 percent believe the Word of God is the literal Word of God. So says a recent Gallup poll. Although fairy tale writers draw inspiration from the Bible, I am here to tell you that the Bible can in no way be compared to *Cinderella, Alice in Wonderland* or *Snow White and the Seven Dwarfs,* in which a wicked queen peers into a "mirror, mirror on the wall" to get assurance that she is the fairest of them all.

There is, however, a supernatural mirror, if you will, that we can look into to get assurance that we are the most cherished of them all. This mirror transforms us from glory to glory. It is called the Bible, the Word of God, Holy Scripture. And its authors, inspired by the Holy Ghost, compared it to a mirror on three occasions. By exploring the Bible as a mirror, we gain a clearer understanding of how to become more like the holiest of all.

> Now the Lord is the Spirit; and where the Spirit of the Lord is, there is liberty. But we all, with unveiled face, beholding as in a mirror the glory of the Lord, are being transformed into the same image from glory to glory, just as by the Spirit of the Lord.
>
> 2 Corinthians 3:17–18

When we look into the Word of God, the mirror, it builds faith, restores hope and inspires love in our hearts for God, ourselves and others. When we turn to the Lord—and when we turn through the pages of His Word seeking His truth— the veil is taken away.

In other words, our minds are renewed. And we are transformed by the renewing of our minds as the Spirit of God supernaturally reveals the Word of God with such clear understanding that we are never the same. Religion fades away. Witchcraft breaks. Jezebel is powerless.

Now, here is the rub. As we look into the mirror that is the Word of God, we must believe what it says about who we are, and we must do what it says we should do by the grace of God. Otherwise, we walk away with a spirit of deception hot on our trails. James said it better than I can:

> But be doers of the word, and not hearers only, deceiving yourselves. For if anyone is a hearer of the word and not a doer, he is like a man observing his natural face in a mirror; for he observes himself, goes away, and immediately forgets what kind of man he was.
>
> James 1:22–24

The mirror tells us who we are:

As Jesus was, so are we in this world (see 1 John 4:17).

We are the righteousness of God in Christ Jesus (see 2 Corinthians 5:21).

We are partakers of His divine nature (see 2 Peter 1:3–4).

We are joint heirs with Christ (see Romans 8:17).

We can know that He who is in us is greater than he who is in the world (see 1 John 4:4).

We can do all things through Christ Jesus (see Philippians 4:13).

We are holy and without blame before Him (see Ephesians 1:4).

We are complete in Him, who is the head of all principality and power (see Colossians 2:10).

We are the head and not the tail, above and not beneath (see Deuteronomy 28:13).

We are more than conquerors in Christ (see Romans 8:37).

We are overcomers by the blood of the Lamb and the word of our testimony (see Revelation 12:11).

We Act Like Who We Think We Are

I could go on and on about who you are in Christ. The mirror speaks clearly. There is an interesting correlation here between our behavior and the revelation of who we are. I believe that when we fail to walk in the revealed light of God's Word to us, we are robbed of the confidence of who we are in Him, and the door is opened to religion, which has a form of godliness but denies its power to change us (see 2 Timothy 3:5).

Sin—failing to do what the Word says—causes a breach in our fellowship with God. It brings guilt, shame and condemnation. When we sin, we have to remember who we are in Christ—the forgiven—and quickly repent. Then we need to go look into the mirror of the Word to ponder more fully who it says we are. The more time we spend in front of the mirror looking at who we are, the less often we will stumble.

A revelation of who we are is a mighty weapon against the deadly trio. When we put that revelation into words, it becomes a spiritual sword. Look out, devil!

Our ultimate goal is to be transformed into the image of Christ. The writer of Hebrews offers us hope:

> Going through a long line of prophets, God has been addressing our ancestors in different ways for centuries. Recently he spoke to us directly through his Son. By his Son, God created the world in the beginning, and it will all belong to the Son at the end. This Son perfectly mirrors God, and is stamped

137

with God's nature. He holds everything together by what he says—powerful words!

Hebrews 1:1–3 MESSAGE

The Son perfectly mirrors God. One day, we will perfectly mirror the Son. Until then, we need to slam the door on religion, Jezebel and witchcraft and open the door to the Holy Spirit to reveal Jesus to us. We need to look into the mirror of God's Word to seek the face of the holiest of all—and speak forth the revelation of who we are in Christ and who we will be in eternity. Powerful words!

Swords That Overcome Religion

I shared with you a slew of Scriptures about who you are in Christ. Ultimately, overcoming the religious spirit in your life boils down to

- having a righteous consciousness rather than a sin consciousness,
- walking in the principles of the Spirit,
- renewing your mind with the Word of God,
- fleeing the scene of sinful temptations,
- surrendering to God.

Here are five spiritual weapons to help you overcome the religious spirit and its running mate Jezebel.

1. Maintain a Righteousness Consciousness

Here is your Sword:

Likewise you also, reckon yourselves to be dead indeed to sin, but alive to God in Christ Jesus our Lord. Therefore do not

138

let sin reign in your mortal body, that you should obey it in its lusts. And do not present your members as instruments of unrighteousness to sin, but present yourselves to God as being alive from the dead, and your members as instruments of righteousness to God.

Romans 6:11–13

You are dead to sin. Keep reminding yourself of that. You are alive to God in Christ. Christ lives in you. Meditate on that. The Holy Spirit dwells in you. You are endowed with power to overcome all the power of the enemy. Act as if you believe it.

2. *Walk by the Principles of the Spirit*

Here is your Sword:

I say then: Walk in the Spirit, and you shall not fulfill the lust of the flesh.

Galatians 5:16

How do you know when you are walking by the principles of the Spirit? Examine the fruit. The works of the flesh are "adultery, fornication, uncleanness, lewdness, idolatry, sorcery, hatred, contentions, jealousies, outbursts of wrath, selfish ambitions, dissensions, heresies, envy, murder, drunkenness, revelries, and the like" (Galatians 5:19–21). By contrast, the fruit of the Spirit is "love, joy, peace, longsuffering, kindness, goodness, faithfulness, gentleness, self-control" (Galatians 5:22–23).

3. *Renew Your Mind Continually*

Here is your Sword:

But you have not so learned Christ, if indeed you have heard Him and have been taught by Him, as the truth is in Jesus:

that you put off, concerning your former conduct, the old man which grows corrupt according to the deceitful lusts, and be renewed in the spirit of your mind, and that you put on the new man which was created according to God, in true righteousness and holiness.

Ephesians 4:20–24

Confess that you are renewed in the spirit of your mind and put on the new man every day, just as you put on your whole armor of God. Saying this another way, meditate on who you are in Christ.

4. Flee the Scene of Sinful Temptations

Here is your Sword:

Flee also youthful lusts; but pursue righteousness, faith, love, peace with those who call on the Lord out of a pure heart.

2 Timothy 2:22

Once you have fled the scene of the lust, you are not through: Pursue something else—namely, righteousness, faith, love and peace. Get your mind off the temptation and onto your Father's business.

5. Surrender to God

Here is your Sword:

Submit to God. Resist the devil and he will flee from you.

James 4:7

When you submit to God—when you submit to the principles of the Word and the Spirit—you are resisting the devil. Lust is not irresistible. When lust comes knocking at the door of your mind, the answer is not to ignore it; the answer is to confront it with the weapons of your warfare, which are not carnal but mighty in God for pulling down strongholds—including lust.

Breaking the Cycle of Religious Bullying

What do you do when confronted by a person who is flowing in a religious spirit, and who wants you to fall in line with its condemning agenda? First, learn to recognize that person as a religious bully. Religious bullies work through tactics like fear, manipulation, sarcasm, coercion, ridicule, cold shoulder, overreacting, blaming, using the Word as a sledgehammer, verbal attacks, gossip and the like. So the first step in dealing with a religious bully is seeing the spirit behind the bully. That is, of course, the religious spirit.

Pray that the religious bully will be set free from the influence of this murdering spirit. Do not get too emotional when a religious bully confronts you—and do not automatically blame yourself. It is not necessarily your fault; you probably have not done anything wrong. Religious bullies have emotional problems of their own, so never engage at the emotional level. Clearly, you are a threat to the religious spirit or you would not be a target.

Do not bully back. It is not worth it. Do not give in to the religious bully's intimidation, either. Ignore the religious bully's tactics if you can. Do not even dignify the bullying with a response. That is what the religious spirit wants—it wants to trap you with your words and make you look like the bad guy. The Pharisees constantly tried to trap Jesus—it never worked.

If the religious bully will not back off, then do not hesitate to stand up for yourself. Jesus put the Pharisees in their places more than once, while refusing to get into a debate. When the religious bullies were abusing Jesus, He asked, "If I have spoken evil, bear witness of the evil; but if well, why do you strike Me?" (John 18:23). Turning the other cheek does not mean becoming a doormat. You can stand up to a religious bully without stooping to his or her level. Oh, and if you are a religious bully, I beseech you, repent, because Jesus has one word for you: *Woe!*

Jezebel and religion sometimes work together but other times seem diametrically opposed to one another. The religious spirit wants you to try to be perfect, while Jezebel gives you many excuses and grace distortions that try to justify why you do not have to be.

Remember, where the Spirit of the Lord is, there is liberty. That does not give you a license to sin, but if you do sin, you do not have to wallow in condemnation. You can repent, declare war on that behavior and continue to fight the good fight of faith.

When we embrace the work of the cross, it leaves no room for religion or Jezebel.

9

Wicked Works of the Flesh

Although much of our battle is in the spirit, our flesh—our carnal nature—has a tendency to cooperate with Jezebel, religion, witchcraft and other enemies of the cross. Indeed, principalities and powers are in the heavenlies, but these forces often move in the realm of works of the flesh.

Paul explained that if we are Holy Spirit–led, we are not under the Law (see Galatians 5:18). Put another way, when we are Holy Spirit–led we walk free from the bondage of legalistic religion. Likewise, when we walk in the Spirit, Jezebel's seduction does not sway us, and we are immune to the powers of witchcraft. But as soon as we begin moving in works of the flesh, we open the door to Satan's deadly trio.

Consider again Paul's words:

> Now the works of the flesh are manifest, which are these; adultery, fornication, uncleanness, lasciviousness, idolatry, witchcraft, hatred, variance, emulations, wrath, strife, seditions, heresies, envyings, murders, drunkenness, revellings, and such like: of the which I tell you before, as I have also

told you in time past, that they which do such things shall not inherit the kingdom of God.

Galatians 5:19–21 KJV

When you examine this list, you can see the markings of Jezebel, religion and witchcraft. Adultery, fornication, uncleanness (from the Greek word *impurity*), lasciviousness (which means "lust") and idolatry are in the realm of Jezebel. Witchcraft is clearly identified. Hatred, strife, wrath, envyings and murder manifest where the religious spirit rules.

The bottom line: We open ourselves to attack—and we open ourselves to being used by the enemy to attack others—when we do not walk in the Spirit. While I have never met anyone who walks in the Spirit all day every day without exception, it is possible to reach depths in the Spirit where you are quick to repent—and, therefore, quick to slam the door in the enemy's face—when you sin.

In this place, you have greater sensitivity to the Holy Spirit. You also have greater sensitivity to spirits that oppose His will, and you can go on the offense in the name of Jesus to overcome them.

Who Has Bewitched You?

Before listing the works of the flesh, Paul offered the Galatians a warning: "Walk in the Spirit, and you shall not fulfill the lust of the flesh. For the flesh lusts against the Spirit, and the Spirit against the flesh; and these are contrary to one another, so that you do not do the things that you wish" (Galatians 5:16–17).

It seems the Galatians were struggling in the battle between works of the Spirit and works of the Law. Some of the Galatians were turning away from Jesus to a different gospel (see Galatians 1:6). Paul told them emphatically that the works of the Law would not justify them (see Galatians 2:16). We know that no flesh shall glory in God's presence (see 1 Corinthians 1:29), but, somehow, the Galatians were falling back into old fleshly habits.

Paul wrote:

> O foolish Galatians! Who has bewitched you that you should not obey the truth, before whose eyes Jesus Christ was clearly portrayed among you as crucified? This only I want to learn from you: Did you receive the Spirit by the works of the law, or by the hearing of faith? Are you so foolish? Having begun in the Spirit, are you now being made perfect by the flesh? Have you suffered so many things in vain—if indeed it was in vain?
>
> Galatians 3:1–4

That word *bewitched* comes from the Greek word *baskaino*, which means "to be charmed, put under a spell or seduced." Now, the word *flesh* in the passage above is rooted in the Greek word *sarx*. *Sarx* relates to the carnal nature. Strong's Concordance defines it as "flesh, body, human nature, materiality." Strong's says it is "generally negative, referring to making decisions (actions) according to self—i.e., apart from faith (independent of God's inworking.) Thus what is 'of the flesh (carnal)' is by definition displeasing to the Lord—even things that seem 'respectable!'"

The Galatians entered into works of the flesh in an effort to go deeper into the Spirit. Specifically, they were trying to keep the Law through their flesh. Christ made them free, but their insistence on keeping the Law was returning them to the bondage of the curse that goes with breaking it. Paul told them: "Stand fast therefore in the liberty by which Christ has made us free, and do not be entangled again with a yoke of bondage. . . . You ran well. Who hindered you from obeying the truth?" (Galatians 5:1, 7).

What had happened? False teachers had crept in and hindered them from obeying the truth of our liberty in Christ. Paul warned them of this danger, while also pointing out the other side:

> Do not use liberty as an opportunity for the flesh, but through love serve one another. For all the law is fulfilled in one word, even in this: "You shall love your neighbor as yourself." But if you bite and devour one another, beware lest you be consumed by one another!
>
> Galatians 5:13–15

Paul told the Galatians to walk in the Spirit so that they would not fulfill the lust of the flesh. He went on to list the works of the flesh, and then discussed the fruit of the Spirit. That is contrasted beautifully with the above words that illustrate love and hate.

The point is this: Works of the flesh open the door to the demonic. You might not be engaging in adultery, fornication or uncleanness, but Jezebel will pounce on lasciviousness (lust) of any kind. You might not be drunk, in sedition or preaching heresy, but idolatry, hatred, strife and envy open you to attack. And keep in mind that Paul did not list every work of the flesh. At the end of the list he said, "And such the like" (Galatians 5:21). Anything that is not produced according to God's Spirit—anything not originating from the motivation of God's love—is of the flesh.

Being Too Quick to Blame the Devil

Spiritual warfare against churches that are making an impact for God can be fierce—sometimes discouraging and sometimes even deadly. I have known some pastors who quit and other pastors who died prematurely in the face of intense battles. Yes, the spiritual warfare is all too real at times.

But can we really blame spirits like Jezebel, witchcraft and religion for all our warfare? In my experience, principalities and powers surely attack, but too often we willfully, if unknowingly, open the front door to every kind of evil.

In my book *The Spiritual Warrior's Guide to Defeating Jezebel* (Chosen, 2013), I explain my first revelation of the Jezebel spirit. Here, again, is that condensed version.

A young man in my church was interested in me romantically, but I did not return the affection. Hoping to spark some sort of twisted competition for his favor, he made up grandiose (and perverted) lies about having a relationship with my best friend. When the truth was exposed, and I made it abundantly clear that he needed to exit my life at all levels, he instead began stalking me.

Eventually, one of the pastors asked him not to return to the church. He was operating in a seducing, controlling spirit and would not receive counsel and repent. He was unstable and it was getting scarier all the time. When I say he was stalking me, I mean it literally. He was under the influence of a Jezebel spirit. It was not the first time Jezebel had targeted me; it was just the first time I understood who the enemy was.

What I now refer to as this "Jezebel revelation" was at first liberating. The Jezebel revelation explained the nature of spiritual attacks I had experienced for decades. When I finally discerned the Jezebelic assignment against my life, evident in this young man's threats, my mouth literally dropped open. In an instant, I understood why the enemy had made it a mission to kill me, steal from me and otherwise bring destruction into my life.

I will be honest. At first I felt somewhat important that Jezebel would pick on "little old me." As I educated myself with what materials I could find on this principality, I grew confident in my ability to identify a Jezebel spirit—and I had the faith to overcome. But before too long, I was unwittingly glorifying Jezebel and I did not even have a full understanding of what I was battling.

While I will always remember the moment I got the revelation of the existence of Jezebel, I will also remember how far out of balance I got with this revelation. As I mentioned, it was liberating to understand that Jezebel was working to steal, kill and destroy through a young man who pretended to befriend me only later to stalk me. When I discovered the name *Jezebel*, I was no longer buffeting the air, so to speak, because I had identified the enemy.

In my immaturity, however, and based on incomplete understanding, I waged war against Jezebel and began to blame this spirit for everything that went wrong in my life. I thought every obstacle was Jezebel. So I went around "binding" that spirit every time something failed to go my way. I rose up against Jezebel in spiritual warfare every time I encountered someone who I thought was trying to control me or manipulate me. I put Jezebel under my feet every morning when I woke up with a list of confessions that aimed to ward her off as if she were some sort of daylight vampire.

When my computer crashed: "I bind you, Jezebel. You nasty witch!" When my tire went flat: "I bind you, Jezebel. You nasty witch!" When I had a bad day: "I bind you, Jezebel. You nasty witch!" Looking back, I see the danger. But this is what I was taught to do by the spiritual leaders around me, who often raised their voices against this evil spirit to the point of becoming hoarse.

I began to realize that this was an exercise in the flesh and reaped no fruit. All the binding never seemed to keep Jezebel at bay. . . .

Jezebel was behind every doorknob. If someone got sick, it was Jezebel's witchcrafts. If someone did not want to come to church, it was Jezebel's imaginations. If someone had a strong opinion that did not agree with the pastor's, it was Jezebel's control.

I learned from that experience that we need balance in spiritual warfare. We need discernment, not witch hunts. It is far too easy to get into the flesh, and you cannot win a battle against the devil by operating in the flesh. Only God can defeat the enemy in our lives. He might use us to speak His word in His name—He might use us as the battle-ax (see Jeremiah 51:20)—but our victory is "not by might nor by power, but by My Spirit" (Zechariah 4:6).

Warfare: A Badge of Honor?

I was once part of a church where we wore the "I'm under attack!" label like a badge of honor. Leadership joked that even attempts to create a flyer for outreach would unleash principalities and powers against them. The not-too-subtle insinuation was that the church was such a threat to the enemy that he dispatched a host of demons to thwart its every step. This church was proud of its warfare. And it was into extremes.

Taking pride in being attacked was the first sign that something was wrong. Pride is not listed as a work of the flesh, but it emanates from the carnal mind. Jesus said,

> "What comes out of a man, that defiles a man. For from within, out of the heart of men, proceed evil thoughts, adulteries, fornications, murders, thefts, covetousness, wickedness, deceit, lewdness, an evil eye, blasphemy, pride, foolishness. All these evil things come from within and defile a man."
>
> Mark 7:20–23

Notice how closely this list resembles the works of the flesh that Paul outlined: adultery, fornication, uncleanness, lasciviousness, idolatry, witchcraft, hatred, variance, emulations, wrath, strife, seditions, heresies, envyings, murders, drunkenness, revellings. When Jesus said that what comes out of the heart of man defiles the man, He was not talking about our spirits—He was talking about the mind governed by the flesh.

Paul wrote: "To be carnally minded is death, but to be spiritually minded is life and peace. Because the carnal mind is enmity against God; for it is not subject to the law of God, nor indeed can be. So then, those who are in the flesh cannot please God" (Romans 8:6–7).

When we take pride in being attacked—or take pride in our spiritual warfare skills—we are setting ourselves up for a fall: "Pride goes before destruction, and a haughty spirit before a fall" (Proverbs 16:18). Pride in spiritual warfare is dangerous because pride interferes with our seeking God (see Psalm 10:4). Wisdom hates pride (see Proverbs 8:12–13). Pride comes from the carnal mind, which makes pride in warfare so dangerous because "the weapons of our warfare are not carnal but mighty in God for pulling down strongholds" (2 Corinthians 10:4). We need God's weapons to pull down strongholds. But God resists the proud (see James 4:6).

Pride is something for which we need to search our hearts and repent frequently, because it is part of our fleshly nature. It defiles us.

Strife: Open Door to the Demonic

Strife is another key part of the fleshly nature that defiles us. When you yield to strife—a work of the flesh—you open the door to the demonic. Strife spreads like wildfire. So, what does strife look like and what causes it? Where you see power struggles and exertion of superiority, you cannot automatically blame Jezebel, witchcraft or religious spirits. Strife is very often the motivator. When you see arguing or contending over anything, it is not always rebellion. Strife is typically lurking nearby. When you see double standards, strife could be at the root.

Strife is an abomination to God (see Proverbs 6:16–19). How can we wield His mighty weapons when we are engaged in an abomination? Strife affects the anointing and the flow of the Holy Ghost (see Psalm 133:1–3). Strife grieves the Holy Spirit (see Ephesians 4:28–30). Strife is rooted in anger (see Proverbs 29:22), hatred (see Proverbs 10:12), pride (see Proverbs 13:10) and a quarrelsome, self-seeking spirit (see Galatians 5:14–18; see also Luke 22:24–27). Strife plays in the field of flesh with all manner of sin.

James put it this way:

> Where do wars and fights come from among you? Do they not come from your desires for pleasure that war in your members? You lust and do not have. You murder and covet and cannot obtain. You fight and war. Yet you do not have because you do not ask. You ask and do not receive, because you ask amiss, that you may spend it on your pleasures.
>
> James 4:1–3

It was James who also said this:

> But if ye have bitter envying and strife in your hearts, glory not, and lie not against the truth. This wisdom descendeth not from above, but is earthly, sensual, devilish. For where envying and strife is, there is confusion and every evil work.
>
> James 3:14–16 KJV

Let me repeat what James wrote so you do not miss it: "Where envying and strife is, there is confusion and every evil work." Strife opens the door to principalities, powers, rulers of the darkness of this age and spiritual hosts of wickedness in the heavenly places. Strife opens the door to spiritual warfare.

If you are under attack, I urge you not to have a knee-jerk reaction. Do not go on a witch hunt for Jezebel. Do not ignore the devil, either, and certainly do not take pride in the fact that the enemy has targeted you for attack.

Instead, get on your face and worship God. Repent of anything He shows you that is not right in your own heart. Then ask Him what the source of the warfare is. It could be Jezebel or any number of spirits coming against you. But it could be internal strife, pride or one of the many other works of the flesh. Never lie against the truth. If works of the flesh are at the root of your spiritual warfare, repent so you can see clearly to battle your other spiritual enemies.

When Good Works Are Witchcraft

Make no mistake. The Spirit of God is against witchcraft in whatever form it takes, from divination to magic to rebellion to word curses—to works of the flesh. Why does the Bible, in Galatians 5:19–20, list witchcraft as one of the works of the flesh? The type of witchcraft Paul is calling out is related to our willpower—a will that stands against God.

When we pray our will rather than God's will—whether it is a curse instead of a blessing or a declaration instead of a prayer of sanctification when we are unsure of God's will—it is a form of fleshly witchcraft. In other words, when we allow our flesh to dictate our words and actions rather than the Spirit—or when we disobey the Word of God to follow our own will—we are tapping in to sorcery. We might have good motives, but if they are not Spirit-led, even "good works" can be works of the flesh that wind up manipulating situations and people to reach the goal.

I once supported a missionary who seemed to be on fire for God. He was certainly passionate about the work of the ministry. But his fundraising mechanisms were not completely honest. He spent a lot of time in the pulpit—time that could have been spent ministering to the congregation—to give updates about his ministry plans and to ask for money. And, as we later learned, he was misrepresenting what the money was being used for.

On one occasion, for instance, he said he was planning a three-week trip to minister in a foreign country and was close to raising all the funds he needed. He asked for financial help to make up the amount. Another ministry in the church, without asking what "close" meant, assumed he needed a few hundred dollars and agreed to make up the difference. That ministry soon learned that he actually needed two thousand dollars. Even worse than that deception, the missionary preached on foreign soil as he promised, but for only three days of the three-week trip. The rest of the money went to a family vacation before and after this three-day mission.

This missionary manipulated the situation to his own benefit, and took seed that people thought they were sowing into souls to spend on his vacation. And he saw nothing wrong with it! He was moving in witchcraft, a work of the flesh, to get what he wanted—which was not necessarily what God wanted.

This does not happen only in ministry situations, of course. In everyday life, people try to control and manipulate us to get what they want—and we have to guard ourselves from doing the same. It is part of our carnal nature to try to get what we want when we want it and how we want it. But we cannot allow people to manipulate and control us—and we cannot manipulate or control others. The consequences are serious.

Again, what are the works of the flesh? Galatians 5:19–21 lists them: "adultery, fornication, uncleanness, lasciviousness, idolatry, witchcraft, hatred, variance, emulations, wrath, strife, seditions, heresies, envyings, murders, drunkenness, revellings, and such like" (kjv). Notice that witchcraft is listed right alongside adultery and murder.

Witchcraft is a serious offense in any manifestation. As a work of the flesh, witchcraft violates the first Commandment: "You shall have no other gods before me." The flesh opposes the move of the Spirit and resists all things spiritual. This is a serious struggle because Paul assures us that those who practice witchcraft will not inherit the Kingdom of God (see Galatians 5:21).

Walking in the Spirit

But there is yet good news: If you walk in the Spirit, you will not fulfill the lusts of the flesh (see Galatians 5:16). How do you know if you are walking in the Spirit? The fruit of the Spirit is love, joy, peace, longsuffering, kindness, goodness, faithfulness, gentleness and self-control. When you walk in the Spirit, this fruit manifests.

So how do we walk in the Spirit? We walk in the Spirit by talking with the Spirit. It is just that simple. When we release simple prayers throughout the day, when we ask the Holy Spirit for insight, when we thank Him and praise Him, we are walking with Him. It is a very simple concept, both to understand and to practice. Usually, it is more a matter of remembering to do it than knowing how.

I have discovered that if we talk to the Holy Spirit, He will talk back to us. Now, He does not always speak with a voice—still, small or otherwise. Many times it is a faint impression, but you know by your spirit that His Spirit is leading you. When you follow that impression, you notice that grace is available to you to overcome an obstacle, complete a task or resist a fleshly urge to violate Scripture.

Mike Bickle, of the International House of Prayer in Kansas City, says, "We will not walk in the Spirit more than we talk to the Spirit." I have found this to be true. Talking with the Spirit throughout the day—asking Him for help as we need it—demonstrates humility, complete dependence on God. God gives grace to the humble. When we talk with the Spirit, we are more likely to obey the Word of God because we are more aware of His presence and not so quick to turn our hearts away from His.

When we thank the Holy Spirit for His power working in us, it opens our hearts to experience more of that transforming power in our lives. So many times we pray for grace or strength when, the truth is, the Spirit of Grace lives within us. If we had a greater awareness of His presence—which we gain by talking with Him—we would have fewer struggles with the flesh and more victories.

Consider these inspiring quotes from Brother Lawrence, a lay brother in a Carmelite monastery in seventeenth-century Paris, from his classic book *The Practice of the Presence of God*:

> That we should establish ourselves in a sense of God's presence, by continually conversing with Him. That it was a shameful thing to quit His conversation, to think of trifles and fooleries.

> A little lifting up of the heart suffices; a little remembrance of God, an interior act of adoration, even though made on the march and with sword in hand, are prayers which, short though they may be, are nevertheless very pleasing to God, and far from making a soldier lose his courage on the most

dangerous occasions, bolster it. Let him then think of God as much as possible so that he will gradually become accustomed to this little but holy exercise; no one will notice it and nothing is easier than to repeat often during the day these little acts of interior adoration.

That we need only to recognize God intimately present with us, to address ourselves to Him every moment, that we may beg His assistance for knowing His will in things doubtful, and for rightly performing those which we plainly see He requires of us, offering them to Him before we do them, and giving Him thanks when we have done.

Take a moment now and thank the Holy Spirit for His presence. Ask Him to help you work out the fruit of the Spirit in your life—love, joy, peace, longsuffering, kindness, goodness, faithfulness, gentleness, self-control. The Spirit of God dwells within you. He is closer to your heart than any other person, and He longs for a relationship with you.

When you focus on the Holy Spirit, His love, His power, His fruit and His beauty, you will come up to entirely new heights in the battle against the flesh—and Jezebel, religion, witchcraft and any other spiritual enemy that tries to attack.

10

Forgiveness: Your Stealth Weapon Against the Enemy

My imagination was running wild. I could not comprehend how someone who claimed to be a Christian could leave town on Christmas Eve without finishing the construction work in my home he had been paid thousands of dollars to complete a month earlier. How could this man leave me in a construction zone without any way to take a shower or cook a meal?

Over and over again, I rehearsed in my mind what I would say to this brother. I would have to wait, of course, because he was off on a wonderful Christmas vacation with his family. I was planning on giving him a piece of my mind. I rehearsed mentally what I would say, imagined how he would respond, planned what I would say next and so on. I was seething mad.

But I was also violating Scripture.

The Bible tells us to cast down "arguments and every high thing that exalts itself against the knowledge of God, bringing every thought into captivity to the obedience of Christ, and being ready to punish all disobedience when your obedience is fulfilled" (2 Corinthians 10:5–6). Instead, I was letting the enemy fill my thoughts and opening the door for witchcraft to attack my mind.

When we meditate on the thoughts the enemy puts into our minds, we are setting ourselves up for destruction. In this case, the enemy was playing on the injustice done to me to set me up for bitterness, resentment and unforgiveness.

I am grateful to say that I caught on to the enemy's plan, and brought those thoughts into captivity to the obedience of Christ, being quick to forgive and trusting God to be my vindicator. Through that experience and others, I learned how to wield the weapon of forgiveness.

Indeed, volumes have been written on forgiveness, but have you ever considered forgiveness as a weapon in spiritual warfare? Forgiveness can set others free from bondages—and prevent you from falling into the bondage of Jezebel, witchcraft and religion (and other spiritual tormenters).

Why Satan's Deadly Trio Is Oppressing You

Consider the parable of the unforgiving servant. When Peter asked Jesus how many times he had to forgive a brother who sinned against him, the answer was "seventy times seven." In other words, over and over and over and over again—endlessly. Jesus then went on to offer a parable, told in Matthew 18:23–34.

"The Kingdom of heaven is like a certain king who wanted to settle accounts with his servants. And when he had begun to settle accounts, one was brought to him who owed him ten thousand talents. But as he was not able to pay, his master commanded that he be sold, with his wife and children and all that he had, and that payment be made. The servant therefore fell down before him, saying, 'Master, have patience with me, and I will pay you all.' Then the master of that servant was moved with compassion, released him, and forgave him the debt.

"But that servant went out and found one of his fellow servants who owed him a hundred denarii; and he laid hands on him and took him by the throat, saying, 'Pay me what you owe!'

"So his fellow servant fell down at his feet and begged him, saying, 'Have patience with me, and I will pay you all.'

"And he would not, but went and threw him into prison till he should pay the debt. So when his fellow servants saw what had been done, they were very grieved, and came and told their master all that had been done.

"Then his master, after he had called him, said to him, 'You wicked servant! I forgave you all that debt because you begged me. Should you not also have had compassion on your fellow servant, just as I had pity on you?'

"And his master was angry, and delivered him to the torturers until he should pay all that was due to him."

Then Jesus warned, "So My heavenly Father also will do to you if each of you, from his heart, does not forgive his brother his trespasses" (Matthew 18:35). Unforgiveness allows torturers—what the King James translation calls tormentors—access to your soul.

Think then: How can you battle Satan's deadly trio when you are in spiritual prison being tortured at the hand of your enemy?

Forgiveness plays a pivotal role in spiritual warfare. Although forgiveness is not some sort of immunity idol, such as you see on reality TV shows, it does offer a layer of protection in the spiritual battle. And without it, you are wide open for enemy infiltration.

Forgiveness may not be listed in the Ephesians 6 armor set, but make no mistake—we must be quick to forgive those the enemy uses against us or we put ourselves in danger of becoming like the spirits we so hate. If bitterness is a root that defiles, forgiveness is a plow that uproots and exposes the defilement.

Why do you think Jesus taught us to forgive daily? The prayer known as the Lord's Prayer, found in Matthew 6:9–13, instructs us to ask for God's forgiveness daily, but also instructs us to forgive others daily. That is because we need God's forgiveness daily—and we need to forgive others daily.

And it is no coincidence that after Jesus taught His disciples this prayer, He went on immediately to teach more about forgiveness: "For if you forgive men their trespasses, your heavenly Father will also forgive you. But if you do not forgive men their trespasses, neither will your Father forgive your trespasses" (Matthew 6:14–15).

How can we go into battle without the forgiveness of the Father to cleanse us from all unrighteousness (common ground with the enemy)? And how can we be led into battle by the Holy Spirit when our souls are embittered toward someone we will not forgive? We have victory in Jesus, but when we walk in unforgiveness we are giving place to the devil (see Ephesians 4:26–27).

Can you see it?

Forgiveness: Your Secret Weapon

If the weapons of our warfare are not carnal—if they are "mighty in God for pulling down strongholds" as Paul described in 2 Corinthians 10:4—then forgiveness may be among your stealthiest weapons. The enemy never sees it coming. Think about it for a minute. God used forgiveness to deliver us from the enemy's camp. All we have to do is repent and receive that forgiveness to remain free from oppression and condemnation the enemy heaps on our souls when we sin. There are two angles worthy of exploration here. First, the enemy often works through people to do his dirty work. As we have discovered through the pages of this book, Jezebel, religion and witchcraft are powerful forces that often work in the realm of imaginations. These spirits can pack an even more powerful punch when they manifest through flesh and blood that launches fiery verbal darts and other manner of persecution.

But there is another angle: When you walk in forgiveness toward others, the enemy cannot put you into bondage to resentment, bitterness and unforgiveness. When you look at forgiveness through this lens, you can see how powerful it is to keep your heart free and clean. Indeed, obeying God's command to forgive opens the door for God to "punish all disobedience" that caused you harm. That includes the deadly trio.

Remember, though, that forgiveness is a double-edged sword. Jesus said that if we do not forgive others, our heavenly Father will not forgive us (see Matthew 6:15). Those are strong words that are hard to swallow. The reality is, however, that unforgiveness hinders your fellowship with God and affects your anointing. You might continue to command devils in the name of Jesus, but authentic spiritual authority is diluted when you fail to obey God's command to love people. Love and unforgiveness cannot flow from the same spring.

If you do not forgive, it will hinder your prayer life. Jesus said, "Whenever you stand praying, if you have anything against anyone, forgive him, that your Father in heaven may also forgive you your trespasses" (Mark 11:25). Spiritual warfare falls under the umbrella of prayer. You cannot effectively bind devils when you yourself are bound with unforgiveness. Unforgiveness puts you at clear disadvantage on the spiritual battlefield. Spiritual warfare is more than binding devils in Jesus' name. Spiritual warfare is forgiving those who oppose you, hurt you or persecute you. And not only forgiving, but also blessing. And not only blessing, but also trusting God to avenge you.

In the Sermon on the Mount, Jesus offered revelation on how to deal with people who mistreat you: "I say to you, love your enemies, bless those who curse you, do good to those who hate you, and pray for those who spitefully use you and persecute you, that you may be sons of your Father in heaven" (Matthew 5:44–45).

It is not possible to apply that revelation if you are not willing to forgive. And Paul wrote:

> Beloved, do not avenge yourselves, but rather give place to wrath; for it is written, "Vengeance is Mine, I will repay," says the Lord. Therefore "If your enemy is hungry, feed him; if he is thirsty, give him a drink; for in so doing you will heap coals of fire on his head." Do not be overcome by evil, but overcome evil with good.
>
> Romans 12:19–21

You might not feel like forgiving. You might feel like giving someone a piece of your mind. You might not feel like blessing your enemy. You might feel like telling the whole town what she did. You might not feel like showing kindness. You may feel like putting your wrath on display. But if you do, you give the enemy a toehold, which can lead to a foothold, which can lead to a stronghold. And before you know it you are being tormented by Jezebel, witchcraft and religion.

The weapon of forgiveness is mighty not only to pull down strongholds, but also to prevent the enemy from establishing a stronghold in the first place. Indeed, forgiveness is a powerful weapon—one that is too often neglected in our binding and loosing exercises.

So before you head to the battlefield, consider that the "Lord is long-suffering and slow to anger, and abundant in mercy and loving-kindness, forgiving iniquity and transgression" (see Numbers 14:18 Amplified). The Lord is a warrior—and He never loses a battle. When you follow His lead and forgive—when you set your heart to overcome evil with good and allow God to take vengeance—you cannot lose.

A Prophetic Warning to Forgive

Long before I knew all of these Scriptures or had any revelation at all on forgiveness—long before I was saved—my great-grandmother gave me a prophetic warning from her deathbed that could very well have saved my life.

When I entered her hospital room, I knew it was the last time I would see her. And she had something important she wanted to tell me. I want to share those same words with you, words with eternal implications. But I first want you to understand the spirit from which they came.

My great-grandmother was born in the 1800s and lived to be nearly one hundred years old. During her lifetime seven states joined the Union. She lived through the women's suffrage and several world-shaking wars. She also lived through the Azusa Street Revival, witnessed the rise of a young Billy Graham and the assassinations of Martin Luther King Jr. and John F. Kennedy.

Mama Norris, as she was affectionately known by hundreds, was also a pillar of the church. She helped plant a handful of churches in the small Florida town she called home. (I still have her Bible in my room and relish reading all of the

Scriptures that she underlined, the Scriptures that touched her heart.)

I said all that to say this: As she lay at the edge of glory, Mama Norris had wisdom equal to and even beyond her 96 years. She had heaven's wisdom in her heart, and she wanted to share it with me. Did she know it was a prophetic admonition that would save my life? I am not sure. But I am sure that the Lord put it on her heart to share three simple yet profound words with me before she came face-to-face with the King.

It was more than twenty years ago that I stood beside her hospital bed knowing she was about to leave this earth. She opened her eyes and saw me standing there. She could not speak above a faint whisper, so she motioned for me to come closer. When I did, she spoke words to me that seemed almost like an inconsequential warning at the time. It would take a decade before I started to understand what she really meant, and another decade before the ultimate revelation graced me.

Here is what she said: "Never hate anyone."

I did not hate anyone at the time. I could not even imagine hating anyone. Not really. Not until my husband abandoned me with a two-year-old child, exiting the country and leaving behind monumental tax issues and credit card bills. My daughter cried every night for a year hoping her missing father might return. He never did. And I hated him. Actually, I hated him with a passion. And I shook my fist at God.

Then I heard those three words Mama told me resonating in my heart: *Never hate anyone.*

Those words saved my eternal life. At the time, I came truly to understand that hating and forgiveness cannot flow out of the same heart. And if I did not forgive my ex-husband, God could not forgive me. But it was not until recently that I got an even greater revelation of Mama's three last words to me.

Unforgiveness Blinds You

I was reading 1 John—a book I have read over and over and over again—and I suddenly received a much deeper understanding of the importance of Mama's words in the light of Scripture:

> He who says he is in the light, and hates his brother, is in darkness until now. He who loves his brother abides in the light, and there is no cause for stumbling in him. But he who hates his brother is in darkness and walks in darkness, and does not know where he is going, because the darkness has blinded his eyes.
>
> 1 John 2:9–11

Mama knew that hate is the ultimate stumbling block. Hate blinds us. Hate was blinding me—and it was opening me to all manner of spiritual attack that I was not equipped to discern. Even if I was equipped to discern it, my unforgiveness would have blinded me to it. I was in bondage.

John, the apostle of love, continues: "We know that we have passed from death to life, because we love the brethren. He who does not love his brother abides in death. Whoever hates his brother is a murderer, and you know that no murderer has eternal life abiding in him" (1 John 3:14–15).

Hate not only blinds us, hate is a sign of murder in our hearts—and a sure sign that eternal life is not dwelling in our spirits. In other words, hatred for mankind cannot live in a heart that belongs to Jesus Christ.

Again, hate had bound me:

> If someone says, "I love God," and hates his brother, he is a liar; for he who does not love his brother whom he has seen, how can he love God whom he has not seen? And this

commandment we have from Him: that he who loves God must love his brother also.

1 John 4:20–21

We are commanded to love. Hatred is a violation of the one new commandment Jesus gave us. If the love of God is shed abroad in our hearts by the Holy Ghost—if it really is—we will draw from His unconditional love to love the unlovely even in the face of their hateful betrayals, vile persecutions and other revolting acts toward us. Hate was killing me.

Love. It is the bottom line of Christianity.

And that was Mama's last effort at preaching the Gospel to her then lost great-grandchild in three forced words from a dying body. Mama wanted to make sure that I would see her one day again in heaven. And God was faithful to raise up a harvest of the word seeds she planted at a time in my life when hatred was trying to lead me into the fiery eternity that is hell. Thanks, Mama. And thank You, Jesus.

Maybe you have never been abandoned or betrayed or persecuted or used or abused. But I reckon you have seen your fair share of mistreatment. Some of you have experienced far worse than I ever will. Or maybe this truth sounds too simple to you, as it did to me when I first heard it. But it is profound, and you might need it one day as I did. (I hope you never do.) Either way, whether you are struggling to forgive right now or could not imagine ever facing such a struggle, I implore you, just as my great-grandmother implored me: "Never hate anyone."

Getting Revenge on the Deadly Trio

Throughout history, people have quipped about revenge. Filmmaker Alfred Hitchcock liked to say, "Revenge is sweet and not fattening." Edward Gibbon stated, "Revenge is profitable; gratitude is expensive." And you have probably heard it said, "I'm coming back with a vengeance."

I have to admit it. I have been tempted to take revenge. Now, I could take justifiable legal action to get unpaid child support, or to force the hand of the brother in Christ who never finished the construction work he was paid to do. But, in my heart, I would be doing those things only out of vengeance, to get even—or to get more than even!—and the Lord makes it emphatically clear that vengeance belongs to Him. He also makes it clear that He will repay (see Romans 12:19).

This means that, despite the emotions that rise up when I am wronged, I believe ultimately that God's vengeance will work out better for me than any attempt I could make to even the score. God sees everything. That is why I reject the quips of Hitchcock and Gibbon in favor of the idea that Roman emperor Marcus Aurelius offered: "The best revenge is to be unlike him who performed the injury." In other words, move in the opposite spirit.

When we take revenge into our own hands—when we try to punish someone who injured us physically, emotionally or financially—we are playing God. More than that, we are not trusting God. More than that, we are tying the hands of a just God who wants to make it up to us. And more than that, we cause our souls greater damage. When we let go of vengeance and decide to forgive, we become more like Christ, we display our trust in God, and we give God free rein to make it up to us.

Would it not be better, then, to come back *without* a vengeance? That is what I have done, and that is what I suggest you do. (I can only suggest we do it, of course; God commands it.) It has been said that living well is the best revenge. It is difficult to live well—or to do much else for God—when we are plotting and planning to swap railing for railing. Jesus said to love and pray for your enemies (see Matthew 5:44). And Peter explained: "Do not repay evil with evil or insult with insult, but with blessing, because to this you were called so that you may inherit a blessing" (1 Peter 3:9 NIV).

The Battle Is the Lord's

When you leave the vengeance to God, there is always a blessing in it. First of all, you are obeying Scripture: "If you are willing and obedient, you shall eat the good of the land" (Isaiah 1:19). Read Deuteronomy 28 for the many blessings that fall upon the obedient. Obey the Lord's command to forgive, and you will be blessed. It is not always easy, but stand on this promise: "Be strong, do not fear! Behold, your God will come with vengeance, with the recompense of God; He will come and save you" (Isaiah 35:4).

When you leave the vengeance to God, you will also see healing and restoration in your life. An old Dutch proverb says, "The tree of revenge does not carry fruit." I disagree. I believe the tree of revenge carries rotten fruit. But the tree of forgiveness yields the fruit of emotional healing. Seventeenth-century British author John Milton put it this way: "He that studieth revenge keepeth his own wounds green, which otherwise would heal and do well." Your emotional well-being is connected to forgiveness, and so is God's justice.

When you leave the vengeance to God, it makes a statement in and of itself. Believe me, when you commit your spirit to God, the people who know the wrong you suffered can discern the difference between the spirit your enemies moved in and the spirit you are moving in.

Let me give you a practical example. About a year after I was sorely persecuted by some believers, several people came to me and said how they knew of the public attacks on the Internet against me—and witnessed how I never retaliated or even defended myself. That spoke volumes about who was moving in the wrong spirit. That, in itself, was vindication enough, but I know God has an even greater repayment in mind.

"An eye for an eye would make the whole world blind," Gandhi said. Indeed, someone has to be the bigger man. Somebody has to be willing to obey God. Somebody has to decide to live the Sermon on the Mount lifestyle—a lifestyle that blesses and prays for the enemy. English philosopher, statesman, scientist, lawyer, jurist, author and pioneer Francis Bacon put it this way: "In taking revenge, a man is but even with his enemy; but in passing it over, he is superior."

God is your vindicator. Vengeance is His. He will repay. Next time you are wronged, launch into prayer. I find Psalm 17 especially helpful: "Hear a just cause, O LORD, attend to my cry; give ear to my prayer which is not from deceitful lips. Let my vindication come from Your presence; let Your eyes look on the things that are upright" (verses 1–2).

And remember this: Living well is the best revenge anyway, and living well means living according to the Word of God. He will take care of the rest.

Break Free from Demonic Curses

Hebrews 12:14–15 says, "Pursue peace with all people, and holiness, without which no one will see the Lord; looking carefully lest anyone fall short of the grace of God; lest any root of bitterness springing up cause trouble, and by this many become defiled." I like *The Message* translation of this verse:

> Work at getting along with each other and with God. Otherwise you'll never get so much as a glimpse of God. Make sure

no one gets left out of God's generosity. Keep a sharp eye out for weeds of bitter discontent. A thistle or two gone to seed can ruin a whole garden in no time.

This strong imagery really drives the point home.

In the Old Testament if a man thought his wife had committed adultery, he brought her to the priest with a jealousy offering. The priest took dust from the floor of the Tabernacle and mixed it into the holy water in an earthen vessel to create "bitter water." The priest uncovered the woman's head, put the jealousy offering in her hands and made her drink the bitter water that brought a curse (see Numbers 5:11–30). If the woman had not committed adultery, then she would go free. But if she had sinned against her husband, then she would be cursed. Her belly would swell, her thigh would rot and she would become a curse among her people.

This is a graphic illustration of Old Testament Law, of course, but the New Testament implications parallel the theme of the ritual. If we drink water embittered by mistreatment, gossip, betrayal or any other wrong brought upon us by Jezebel, religion and witchcraft, then we muddy the streams of living water that are supposed to flow from our bellies.

It is vital that believers not commit adultery with Jezebel and religion by compromising with these spirits. But it is just as vital to forgive the people flowing in these spirits who cause us harm, because Jesus commands us to forgive. Holding on to unforgiveness is like drinking the priest's mixture of bitter water and hoping our enemy's belly will swell. It does not work that way.

Again, deciding to forgive those who have persecuted you with Jezebelic, religious witchcraft attacks keeps your heart pure. But it can also set Jezebel's puppets free. Walking in forgiveness—demonstrating God's love by praying for those who despitefully use you—is sowing the seeds of deliverance in a person's life. Walking in forgiveness—returning good for evil—can heap coals of fire on your enemy's head. What are those coals of fire? I believe it is conviction that could lead them to repentance. And that is our ultimate goal in spiritual warfare—to see the captives set free. Amen.

11

Wrestling with Satan's Deadly Trio

It took me years to get the revelation on the spirits of Jezebel, witchcraft and religion—how they work individually and how they work collectively. It took years, in part, because most churches do not teach about this realm of spiritual warfare. It took years, in part, because there is so much incomplete, copycat teaching in the Body of Christ on these spirits. It took years, in part, because I focused on one spirit at a time and was largely blind to the collaborative strategies of these demons—until the Holy Spirit showed me this malicious menace in operation against me.

Now, you have much of the same knowledge I have—but you still need the Holy Spirit to give you discernment on what you are dealing with. You cannot rely on book knowledge alone to win a battle. You need the Word of God and the Spirit of God to overcome the enemies that rage against your soul. I do, though, want to leave you with a few additional practical nuggets as you stay alert and vigilant about Satan's deadly trio working in your midst.

First, let's review the big picture.

- You have been equipped to see clearly how this sinister spiritual trio operates in direct opposition to the Holy Trinity.
- You have studied examples of how Jezebel seduces God's people into sexual immorality and idolatry—and how it relies on the spirits of religion and witchcraft to aid its nefarious agenda.
- You have read personal stories, showing how witchcraft comes against your mind to enslave you once again with a demonic yoke of oppression—and how to break free from its grip.
- You have seen illustrations of how religion hinders your relationship with Jesus and distorts your view of who you are in Christ—and who He is in you.
- You have received tools from the Gospel tool chest to combat these enemies of your soul in this spiritual war—including the all-important weapon of forgiveness.

Going After the Strongman

Now that you know there is a treacherous tag team working to sabotage you, you can begin to look for the ways these spirits are moving in tandem against your life. I am certainly not suggesting you go on a witch hunt for these spirits, or assume there is a devil behind every door.

Quite the contrary! That is how spiritual warriors get out of balance. Everything is not a devil—and everything is not Jezebel, witchcraft or religion. With this new revelation at hand, you might be tempted to think that everything you are seeing operate is one of these spirits. Do not fall into that ditch!

What I am saying is this: When you are facing opposition—spiritual resistance, imaginations slamming attacks against your mind, attacks against your physical body, your finances, your relationships and so on—consider how these spirits might be contributing to the warfare. Ask the Holy Spirit what is going on—and remember that where you find one of these spirits, you will often find the others.

When, for example, you believe you are under attack from Jezebel, look for witchcraft and religion. Where religion is ruling, look for Jezebel's fingerprints and witchcraft's work. And when you run up against spiritual witchcraft, understand that Jezebel is likely behind it.

But, still, *never assume*. And remember, too, that one of these spirits often looks like another. Indeed, many spirits share common traits, which is why so many people miss them. They play guessing games, deduce or work from a checklist. Those approaches might be helpful in some cases, but there is nothing more accurate than Holy Spirit discernment.

Do not take this book as the "be all and end all" manual for battling these spirits. I have shared with you not only examples of how these spirits operate together, but also my personal battles and the application of Scripture. You probably have stories of your own to share, and others in your life will have wisdom to help you also. Again, there is no checklist that will give you the answers you need in battle, but the Holy Spirit will pick up this teaching where I have left off and allow you to discern, if you will press in to His wisdom.

Often, dealing with demonic spirits is like untying a big knot. You have to pick your way through one tangle before you can deal with another tangle further in. Ultimately, you need to go after the strongman—but usually you have to deal with the lower-level spirits first. Just as Goliath had an armor bearer who spoke words of fear, the strongman often has demonic armor bearers to distract you from locating its hiding place.

Jezebel, religion and witchcraft are often united, but remember that a house divided cannot stand. After the religious Pharisees accused Jesus of casting out devils by Beelzebub, the ruler of demons, Jesus said:

> "Every kingdom divided against itself is brought to desolation, and every city or house divided against itself will not stand. If Satan casts out Satan, he is divided against himself. How then will his kingdom stand? And if I cast out demons by Beelzebub, by whom do your sons cast them out? Therefore they shall be your judges. But if I cast out demons by the Spirit of God, surely the kingdom of God has come upon you. Or how can one enter a strong man's house and plunder his goods, unless he first binds the strong man? And then he will plunder his house. He who is not with Me is against Me, and he who does not gather with Me scatters abroad."
>
> Matthew 12:25–30

Rest assured that every kingdom divided against itself is brought to desolation. Although Jezebel, witchcraft and religion are often united for the common goal of stealing, killing and destroying (see John 10:10), each of these sinister spirits, ultimately, is just as prideful as Satan himself, and seeks its own glory. I believe that our spiritual enemies are often enemies to each other. Can you imagine the competition for glory in the kingdom of darkness?

Let's look at a couple of key instances of how God uses this demonic self-seeking against the enemy and for our benefit.

Confusion in the Enemy's Camp

Jehoshaphat, king of Judah, was facing a great multitude coming against his nation from beyond the sea. You can read the entire account in 2 Chronicles 20, but I will summarize the story here. The news startled him, and he did what every one of us should do when we sense the enemy coming against us: "And Jehoshaphat feared, and set himself to seek the Lord, and proclaimed a fast throughout all Judah. So Judah gathered together to ask help from the Lord; and from all the cities of Judah they came to seek the Lord" (2 Chronicles 20:3–4).

Jehoshaphat set himself to seek the Lord. He also proclaimed a fast. Fasting can be a key strategy in spiritual warfare, because when you put your flesh under submission to your spirit, you become more sensitive to the things of the spirit.

You are a spirit. You have a soul, and you live in a body. By dying to self through fasting, you can also prepare your heart better to break any agreement with the enemy in your soul. There are entire books on fasting and its benefits, so I will not continue down that path. But I would recommend seeking the Lord and even fasting if you are facing intense spiritual warfare and need answers.

Then Jehoshaphat stood in the great assembly and poured out his heart in prayer to God for help. In response, the Spirit of God came upon one of the prophets, and the people heard these words, which have become a touchstone of hope for many:

"Thus says the Lord to you: 'Do not be afraid nor dismayed because of this great multitude, for the battle is not yours, but God's. . . . You will not need to fight in this battle. Position yourselves, stand still and see the salvation of the Lord, who is with you, O Judah and Jerusalem!' Do not fear or be dismayed; tomorrow go out against them, for the Lord is with you."

2 Chronicles 20:15, 17

When the Israelites obeyed the prophetic word, singing praises to God's name, look what happened:

> Now when they began to sing and to praise, the LORD set ambushes against the people of Ammon, Moab, and Mount Seir, who had come against Judah; and they were defeated. For the people of Ammon and Moab stood up against the inhabitants of Mount Seir to utterly kill and destroy them. And when they had made an end of the inhabitants of Seir, they helped to destroy one another.
>
> 2 Chronicles 20:22–23

Look at these same verses in *The Message*:

> As soon as they started shouting and praising, God set ambushes against the men of Ammon, Moab, and Mount Seir as they were attacking Judah, and they all ended up dead. The Ammonites and Moabites mistakenly attacked those from Mount Seir and massacred them. Then, further confused, they went at each other, and all ended up killed.

God sent confusion into the enemy's camp! And this is not the only witness to this heavenly strategy against the enemy. Gideon has a similar testimony in Judges.

Let me give you the background. The enemy here was the Midianites, who were mighty in battle. Gideon had mustered an army, but God told him there were too many warriors with him. Gideon must have been scratching his head about that one, but the point was that God did not want Gideon's army to take credit for the rout.

That is an important point for spiritual warriors. When we are victorious in spiritual warfare, it is God who gives us the victory through Christ. We can take no credit. God will not let another touch His glory. God whittled Gideon's army down to a mere three hundred soldiers before assuring him that the Midianites would be delivered into his hand.

Let's listen in to the conclusion of the battle:

> Then the three companies [of one hundred soldiers each] blew the trumpets and broke the pitchers—they held the torches in their left hands and the trumpets in their right hands for blowing—and they cried, "The sword of the LORD and of Gideon!"
>
> And every man stood in his place all around the camp; and the whole army ran and cried out and fled. When the three hundred blew the trumpets, the LORD set every man's sword against his companion throughout the whole camp; and the army fled to Beth Acacia, toward Zererah, as far as the border of Abel Meholah, by Tabbath.
>
> Judges 7:20–22

Need a third witness? The Lord told the Israelites He would throw their enemies into confusion before they ever entered the Promised Land:

> The LORD your God will drive those nations out ahead of you little by little. You will not clear them away all at once, otherwise the wild animals would multiply too quickly for you. But the Lord your God will hand them over to you. He will throw them into complete confusion until they are destroyed. He will put their kings in your power, and you will erase their names from the face of the earth. No one will be able to stand against you, and you will destroy them all.
>
> Deuteronomy 7:22–24 NLT

Can you see it? You can be assured that if you follow the spiritual blueprint God gives you for victory over your enemies, He will give you the victory. You will win, one way or another.

Dividing Satan's Kingdom

Now, let's get back to targeting the strongman. You cannot deduce anything about the strongman. The strongman has to be discerned. Jesus asked, "How can one enter a strong man's house and plunder his goods, unless he first binds the strong man? And then he will plunder his house" (Matthew 12:29). Luke's gospel expounds on Jesus' words in this incident, explaining, "For when a strong man like Satan is fully armed and guards his palace, his possessions are safe—until someone even stronger attacks and overpowers him, strips him of his weapons, and carries off his belongings" (Luke 11:21–22 NLT).

Jesus, of course, is the stronger one! And you are the stronger one in Him. But that does not mean that you can run up against the strongman in your own flesh.

I have said it over and over and over again, but I never get tired of reminding you. *You cannot wage spiritual warfare with your intellect.* You cannot depend on deduction. You need the Holy Spirit's mind on the matter. You need discernment. The strongman might very well be religion. It might be Jezebel. It might be fear. It might be lust. But it also might be something else you have never encountered before. You could be wasting your energy, spinning your wheels—and, as Paul the apostle said, buffeting the air—by going after the wrong spirit. You could also be picking a fight with a spirit that was not even harassing you!

Demon spirits often share similar characteristics, and, again, work together to accomplish a goal. You have to untangle the spiritual knot to take down the strongman because layers and layers of demonic string sometimes protect the core. If you pull the wrong string, the knot can get tighter instead of looser. As I have suggested, you could possibly open a door to warfare you are not ready to handle by pulling the wrong strings. Do as Jehoshaphat did: Seek the Lord; call a fast; and then wait on Him. When He shows you what to do, do it. Then you are assured the victory.

Remember, the kingdom of darkness is all about division. Demons work to divide your heart from God's heart—to divide your thinking from God's truth. Although the kingdom of darkness is highly organized, I do not believe there is true unity among the principalities, powers, rulers of the darkness of this age and spiritual hosts of wickedness in the heavenly places (see Ephesians 6:12). Just as Lucifer wanted to be exalted above Father God, I believe Satan's demons want to be exalted in their own right. After all, they have a rebellious nature, or they would not have followed him in his insurrection against the Almighty to begin with.

In spiritual warfare, one of your jobs as a blood-bought child of God is to rightly divide the word of truth. As Paul told Timothy, "Be diligent to present yourself approved to God, a worker who does not need to be ashamed, rightly dividing the word of truth. But shun profane and idle babblings, for they will increase to more ungodliness" (2 Timothy 2:15–17). If you do not rightly divide the word of truth when it comes to spiritual warfare, you will potentially open the door to onslaughts you were not expecting, engage in battle with the wrong enemy and wind up defeated.

Throughout this book, I showed you a few of your enemies and how they work together. But, again, dig this out in Scripture for yourself and seek the Holy Spirit's discernment and timing before running to the battle line.

Here is a prayer that I believe will help you.

Spiritual Warrior's Prayer

Father, I thank You that You have sent me another Comforter, the Holy Spirit, to lead me and guide me into all truth—even truth about the enemies that are rising up against me. I ask You, Father, to give me wisdom and understanding in the realm of the spirit. Help me to discern the enemies that are battling against my soul. Let me not move in presumption against what I think I see, but let me move in Christ's confidence against what I know I see because You have revealed it to me.

Show me Your blueprint, Your battle plan—for I will not move forward to bind and loose or root out or overthrow until You show me the way. I thank You for the authority You have given me in Christ. Help me use it wisely in every area of my life.

Now, Father, I plead the blood of Jesus over myself, my family and all that pertains to me. I thank You for Your protection as I enter into a new level of spiritual warfare. I thank You that if I follow Your Spirit, You will always lead me into triumph in Christ.

In the name of Jesus, Amen!

Index

Jennifer LeClaire is director of Awakening House of Prayer in Fort Lauderdale, Florida. Jennifer also serves as news editor of *Charisma* magazine. Her work has appeared in a Charisma House book entitled *Understanding the Fivefold Ministry*, which offers a biblical study of the true purpose of the fivefold ministry, and *The Spiritual Warfare Bible*. Some of Jennifer's work is archived in the Flower Pentecostal Heritage Center museum in Springfield, Missouri.

Jennifer is a prolific author who has written several books, including *The Spiritual Warrior's Guide to Defeating Jezebel*; *The Making of a Prophet*; *The Heart of the Prophetic*; *A Prophet's Heart*; *Fervent Faith*; *Did the Spirit of God Say That?*; *Breakthrough!*; and *Doubtless: Faith That Overcomes the World*. Her materials have been translated into Spanish and Korean.

You can find Jennifer online at www.jenniferleclaire.org or on Facebook at facebook.com/propheticbooks.